PRESENTED TO: _NiCOle_

FROM: _Ernst_

DATE: _bdd ffeihstein_

A Heart Of Gratitude

100 Devotions for a Woman's Heart

The quoted ideas expressed in this book (but not Scripture verses) are not, in all cases, exact quotations, as some have been edited for clarity and brevity. In all cases, the author has attempted to maintain the speaker's original intent. In some cases, quoted material for this book was obtained from secondary sources, primarily print media. While every effort was made to ensure the accuracy of these sources, the accuracy cannot be guaranteed. For additions, deletions, corrections, or clarifications in future editions of this text, please write Freeman-Smith, LLC.

The Holy Bible, King James Version

The Holy Bible, New King James Version (NKJV) Copyright © 1982 by Thomas Nelson, Inc. Used by permission.

New Century Version®. (NCV) Copyright © 1987, 1988, 1991 by Word Publishing, a division of Thomas Nelson, Inc. All rights reserved. Used by permission.

The Holman Christian Standard Bible™ (Holman CSB) Copyright © 1999, 2000, 2001 by Holman Bible Publishers. Used by permission.

The Holy Bible, New International Version®. (NIV) Copyright © 1973, 1978, 1984 International Bible Society. Used by permission of Zondervan. All rights reserved.

The Holy Bible. New Living Translation (NLT) copyright © 1996 Tyndale Charitable Trust. Used by permission of Tyndale House Publishers.

The New American Standard Bible®, (NASB) Copyright © 1960, 1962, 1963, 1968, 1971, 1972, 1973, 1975, 1977, 1995 by The Lockman Foundation. Used by permission.

Scripture taken from The Message. (MSG) Copyright © 1993, 1994, 1995, 1996, 2000, 2001, 2002. Used by permission of NavPress Publishing Group.

Cover Design by Kim Russell / Wahoo Designs
Page Layout by Bart Dawson

ISBN 978-1-60587-260-5

A Heart Of Gratitude

100 Devotions for a Woman's Heart

Introduction

Any time is the right time to express your gratitude to God. But, sometimes, feelings of gratitude may be difficult for you. After all, it isn't easy being a godly woman in today's troubled world. Never have expectations been higher, never have temptations been stronger, never have distractions been so plentiful, and never have demands been greater. Thankfully, God stands ready, willing, and able to help you in every facet of your life if you ask Him. But it's important to remember that the best way to ask God for His help—and the best time to praise Him—is early and often.

The fabric of daily life is woven together with the threads of habit, and no habit is more important than that of consistent prayer and daily devotion to the Creator. And this book is intended to help. This text contains 100 chapters; during the next 100 days, please try this experiment: read a chapter each day. If you're already committed to a daily worship time, this book will enrich that experience. If you are not, the simple act of giving God a few minutes each morning will change the direction and the quality of your life.

This text addresses topics of particular interest to you, a Christian woman living in an uncertain world. If you take the time to meditate upon these devotional readings, you will be reminded of God's love, of His Son, and of His promises. May these pages be a blessing to you, and may you, in turn, be a blessing to your family, to your friends, and to the world.

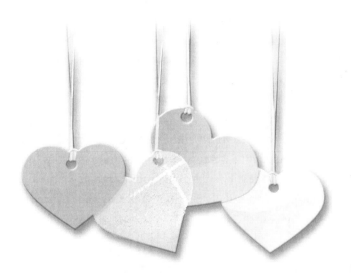

Giving Thanks to the Creator

In everything give thanks; for this is the will of God in Christ Jesus for you.

1 Thessalonians 5:18 NKJV

As believing Christians, we are blessed beyond measure. God sent His only Son to die for our sins. And, God has given us the priceless gifts of eternal love and eternal life. We, in turn, are instructed to approach our Heavenly Father with reverence and thanksgiving. But, as busy women caught up in the inevitable demands of everyday life, we sometimes fail to pause and thank our Creator for the countless blessings He has bestowed upon us.

When we slow down and express our gratitude to the One who made us, we enrich our own lives and the lives of our loved ones. Thanksgiving should become a habit, a regular part of our daily routines. Yes, God has blessed us beyond measure, and we owe Him everything, including our eternal praise.

A Heart of Gratitude

Enter into his gates with thanksgiving, and into his courts with praise: be thankful unto him, and bless his name. For the LORD is good; his mercy is everlasting; and his truth endureth to all generations.

Psalm 100:4-5 KJV

The act of thanksgiving
is a demonstration of the fact
that you are going to trust
and believe God.

—

Kay Arthur

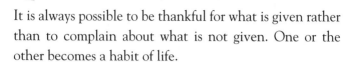
It is always possible to be thankful for what is given rather than to complain about what is not given. One or the other becomes a habit of life.

Elisabeth Elliot

The ability to rejoice in any situation is a sign of spiritual maturity.

Billy Graham

Jesus intended for us to be overwhelmed by the blessings of regular days. He said it was the reason he had come: "I am come that they might have life, and that they might have it more abundantly."

Gloria Gaither

A child of God should be a visible beatitude for joy and a living doxology for gratitude.

C. H. Spurgeon

Today's Prayer

Heavenly Father, Your gifts are greater than I can imagine. May I live each day with thanksgiving in my heart and praise on my lips. Thank You for the gift of Your Son and for the promise of eternal life. Let me share the joyous news of Jesus Christ, and let my life be a testimony to His love and His grace. Amen

Putting God First

Do not have other gods besides Me.

Exodus 20:3 HCSB

As you think about the nature of your relationship with God, remember this: you will always have some type of relationship with Him—it is inevitable that your life must be lived in relationship to God. The question is not if you will have a relationship with Him; the burning question is whether that relationship will be one that seeks to honor Him . . . or not.

Are you willing to place God first in your life? And, are you willing to welcome Him into your heart? Unless you can honestly answer these questions with a resounding yes, then your relationship with God isn't what it could be or should be. Thankfully, God is always available, He's always ready to forgive, and He's waiting to hear from you now. The rest, of course, is up to you.

A Heart of Gratitude

It is good to give thanks to the Lord, and to sing praises to Your name, O Most High; to declare Your lovingkindness in the morning, and Your faithfulness every night.

Psalm 92:1-2 NKJV

11

Love has its source in God,
for love is the very essence
of His being.

—

Kay Arthur

It is when we come to the Lord in our nothingness, our powerlessness and our helplessness that He then enables us to love in a way which, without Him, would be absolutely impossible.

Elisabeth Elliot

When all else is gone, God is still left. Nothing changes Him.

Hannah Whitall Smith

Choose the opposition of the whole world rather than offend Jesus.

Thomas à Kempis

If we are ever going to be or do anything for our Lord, now is the time.

Vance Havner

Today's Prayer

Dear Lord, Your love is eternal and Your laws are everlasting. When I obey Your commandments, I am blessed. Today, I invite You to reign over every corner of my heart. I will have faith in You, Father. I will sense Your presence; I will accept Your love; I will trust Your will; and I will praise You for the Savior of my life: Your Son Jesus. Amen

Gratitude for This Day

We must do the works of Him who sent Me while it is day. Night is coming when no one can work.

John 9:4 HCSB

The words of John 9:4 remind us that "night is coming" for all of us. But until then, God gives us each day and fills it to the brim with possibilities. The day is presented to us fresh and clean at midnight, free of charge, but we must beware: Today is a non-renewable resource—once it's gone, it's gone forever. Our responsibility, of course, is to use this day in the service of God's will and in accordance with His commandments.

Today is a priceless gift that has been given to you by God—don't waste it. Don't stand on the sidelines as life's parade passes you by. Instead, search for the hidden possibilities that God has placed along your path. This day is a one-of-a-kind treasure that can be put to good use—or not. Your challenge is to use this day joyfully and productively. And while you're at it, encourage others to do likewise. After all, night is coming when no one can work . . .

A Heart of Gratitude

This is the day the LORD has made; let us rejoice and be glad in it.

Psalm 118:24 NIV

Christ is the secret, the source, the substance, the center, and the circumference of all true and lasting gladness.

Mrs. Charles E. Cowman

God gave you this glorious day. Don't disappoint Him. Use it for His glory.

Marie T. Freeman

Submit each day to God, knowing that He is God over all your tomorrows.

Kay Arthur

Yesterday is the tomb of time, and tomorrow is the womb of time. Only now is yours.

R. G. Lee

Live today fully, expressing gratitude for all you have been, all you are right now, and all you are becoming.

Melodie Beattie

Today's Prayer

Dear Lord, You have given me another day of life, and I will celebrate it. I will try to live each moment to the fullest as I give thanks for Your creation, for Your love, and for Your Son. Amen

Study His Word

You will be a good servant of Christ Jesus, nourished by the words of the faith and of the good teaching that you have followed.

1 Timothy 4:6 HCSB

God's Word is unlike any other book. The Bible is a roadmap for life here on earth and for life eternal. As Christians, we are called upon to study God's Holy Word, to trust its promises, to follow its commandments, and to share its Good News with the world.

As women who seek to follow in the footsteps of the One from Galilee, we must study the Bible and meditate upon its meaning for our lives. Otherwise, we deprive ourselves of a priceless gift from our Creator. God's Holy Word is, indeed, a transforming, life-changing, one-of-a-kind treasure. And, a passing acquaintance with the Good Book is insufficient for Christians who seek to obey God's Word and to understand His will.

Gratitude for God's Word

Your word is a lamp to my feet and a light to my path.

Psalm 119:105 NKJV

Weave the unveiling fabric of God's word through your heart and mind. It will hold strong, even if the rest of life unravels.

—

Gigi Graham Tchividjian

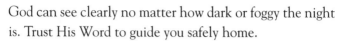

God can see clearly no matter how dark or foggy the night is. Trust His Word to guide you safely home.

Lisa Whelchel

Words fail to express my love for this holy Book, my gratitude for its author, for His love and goodness. How shall I thank him for it?

Lottie Moon

The Bible became a living book and a guide for my life.

Vonette Bright

Study the Bible and observe how the persons behaved and how God dealt with them. There is explicit teaching on every condition of life.

Corrie ten Boom

Today's Prayer

Dear Lord, the Bible is Your gift to me; let me use it. When I stray from Your Holy Word, Lord, I suffer. But, when I place Your Word at the very center of my life, I am blessed. Make me a faithful student of Your Word so that I might be a faithful servant in Your world, this day and every day. Amen

Praying for Spiritual Growth

Rejoice in hope; be patient in affliction; be persistent in prayer.
Romans 12:12 HCSB

On his second missionary journey, Paul started a small church in Thessalonica. A short time later, he penned a letter that was intended to encourage the new believers at that church. Today, almost 2,000 years later, 1 Thessalonians remains a powerful, practical guide for Christian living.

In his letter, Paul advised members of the new church to "pray without ceasing." His advice applies to Christians of every generation. When we consult God on an hourly basis, we avail ourselves of His wisdom, His strength, and His love. As Corrie ten Boom observed, "Any concern that is too small to be turned into a prayer is too small to be made into a burden."

Today, instead of turning things over in your mind, turn them over to God in prayer. Instead of worrying about your next decision, ask God to lead the way. Don't limit your prayers to meals or bedtime. Become a woman of constant prayer. God is listening, and He wants to hear from you. Now.

Gratitude for the Gift of Prayer

Therefore, let everyone who is godly pray to You.

Psalm 32:6 NASB

Repentance removes old sins and wrong attitudes, and it opens the way for the Holy Spirit to restore our spiritual health.

Shirley Dobson

God gives us permission to forget our past and the understanding to live our present. He said He will remember our sins no more. (Psalm 103:11-12)

Serita Ann Jakes

When we reach the end of our strength, wisdom, and personal resources, we enter into the beginning of his glorious provisions.

Patsy Clairmont

God specializes in things fresh and firsthand. His plans for you this year may outshine those of the past. He's prepared to fill your days with reasons to give Him praise.

Joni Eareckson Tada

Obedience is the master key to effective prayer.

Billy Graham

Each of us has something broken in our lives: a broken promise, a broken dream, a broken marriage, a broken heart...and we must decide how we're going to deal with our brokenness. We can wallow in self-pity or regret, accomplishing nothing and having no fun or joy in our circumstances; or we can determine with our will to take a few risks, get out of our comfort zone, and see what God will do to bring unexpected delight in our time of need.

Luci Swindoll

In those desperate times when we feel like we don't have an ounce of strength, He will gently pick up our heads so that our eyes can behold something—something that will keep His hope alive in us.

Kathy Troccoli

Prayer may not get us what we want, but it will teach us to want what we need.

Vance Havner

Today's Prayer

Dear Lord, make me a woman of constant prayer. Your Holy Word commands me to pray without ceasing. In all things great and small, at all times, whether happy or sad, let me seek Your wisdom and Your strength . . . in prayer. Amen

Follow Him

If anyone serves Me, let him follow Me; and where I am, there My servant will be also. If anyone serves Me, him My Father will honor.

John 12:26 NKJV

Jesus walks with you. Are you walking with Him? Hopefully, you will choose to walk with Him today and every day of your life.

Jesus loved you so much that He endured unspeakable humiliation and suffering for you. How will you respond to Christ's sacrifice? Will you take up His cross and follow Him (Luke 9:23), or will you choose another path? When you place your hopes squarely at the foot of the cross, when you place Jesus squarely at the center of your life, you will be blessed. If you seek to be a worthy disciple of Jesus, you must acknowledge that He never comes "next." He is always first.

Do you hope to fulfill God's purpose for your life? Do you seek a life of abundance and peace? Do you intend to be Christian, not just in name, but in deed? Then follow Christ. Follow Him by picking up His cross today and every day that you live. When you do, you will quickly discover that Christ's love has the power to change everything, including you.

A Heart of Gratitude

My cup runs over. Surely goodness and mercy shall follow me all the days of my life; and I will dwell in the house of the Lord forever.

Psalm 23:5-6 NKJV

The love life of the Christian is a crucial battleground. There, if nowhere else, it will be determined who is Lord: the world, the self, and the devil—or the Lord Christ.

Elisabeth Elliot

Will you, with a glad and eager surrender, hand yourself and all that concerns you over into his hands? If you will do this, your soul will begin to know something of the joy of union with Christ.

Hannah Whitall Smith

Today's Prayer

Dear Jesus, because I am Your disciple, I will trust You, I will obey Your teachings, and I will share Your Good News. You have given me life abundant and life eternal, and I will follow You today and forever. Amen

The Power of Perseverance

But thanks be to God, who gives us the victory through our Lord Jesus Christ. Therefore, my beloved brethren, be steadfast, immovable, always abounding in the work of the Lord, knowing that your labor is not in vain in the Lord.

1 Corinthians 15:57-58 NKJV

A well-lived life is like a marathon, not a sprint—it calls for preparation, determination, and, of course, lots of perseverance. As an example of perfect perseverance, we Christians need look no further than our Savior, Jesus Christ.

Jesus finished what He began. Despite His suffering and despite the shame of the cross, Jesus was steadfast in His faithfulness to God. We, too, must remain faithful, especially during times of hardship. Sometimes, God may answer our prayers with silence, and when He does, we must patiently persevere.

Are you facing a tough situation? If so, remember this: whatever your problem, God can handle it. Your job is to keep persevering until He does.

A Heart of Gratitude

Don't be impatient for the Lord to act! Travel steadily along his path. He will honor you....

Psalm 37:34 NLT

Failure is one of life's most
powerful teachers.
How we handle our failures
determines whether we're going
to simply "get by" in life
or "press on."

—

Beth Moore

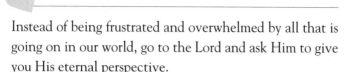

Instead of being frustrated and overwhelmed by all that is going on in our world, go to the Lord and ask Him to give you His eternal perspective.

Kay Arthur

Keep adding, keep walking, keep advancing; do not stop, do not turn back, do not turn from the straight road.

St. Augustine

Perseverance is more than endurance. It is endurance combined with absolute assurance and certainty that what we are looking for is going to happen.

Oswald Chambers

We are all on our way somewhere. We'll get there if we just keep going.

Barbara Johnson

Today's Prayer

Lord, when life is difficult, I am tempted to abandon hope in the future. But You are my God, and I can draw strength from You. Let me trust You, Father, in good times and in bad times. Let me persevere—even if my soul is troubled—and let me follow Your Son, Jesus Christ, this day and forever. Amen

Your Daily Devotional

He awakens Me morning by morning, He awakens My ear to hear as the learned. The Lord God has opened My ear.

Isaiah 50:4-5 NKJV

Each new day is a gift from God, and if we are wise, we will spend a few quiet moments each morning thanking the Giver. Daily life is woven together with the threads of habit, and no habit is more important to our spiritual health than the discipline of daily prayer and devotion to the Creator.

When we begin each day with our heads bowed and hearts lifted, we remind ourselves of God's love, His protection, and His commandments. And if we are wise, we align our priorities for the coming day with the teachings and commandments that God has given us through His Holy Word.

Are you seeking to change some aspect of your life? Do you seek to improve the condition of your spiritual or physical health? If so, ask for God's help and ask for it many times each day . . . starting with your morning devotional.

Gratitude for God's Guidance

Seek the LORD and His strength; seek His face continually.

Psalm 105:4 NASB

Jesus challenges you and me
to keep our focus daily
on the cross of His will
if we want to be His disciples.

—

Anne Graham Lotz

I suggest you discipline yourself to spend time daily in a systematic reading of God's Word. Make this "quiet time" a priority that nobody can change.

Warren Wiersbe

A person with no devotional life generally struggles with faith and obedience.

Charles Stanley

Think of this—we may live together with Him here and now, a daily walking with Him who loved us and gave Himself for us.

Elisabeth Elliot

I believe the reason so many are failing today is that they have not disciplined themselves to read God's Word consistently, day in and day out, and to apply it to every situation in life.

Kay Arthur

Today's Prayer

Dear Lord, every day of my life is a journey with You. I will take time today to think, to pray, and to study Your Word. Guide my steps, Father, and keep me mindful that today offers yet another opportunity to celebrate Your blessings, Your love, and Your Son. Amen

Entrusting Your Hopes to God

You, Lord, give true peace to those who depend on you, because they trust you.

Isaiah 26:3 NCV

As every woman knows, hope is a perishable commodity. Despite God's promises, despite Christ's love, and despite our countless blessings, we frail human beings can still lose hope from time to time. When we do, we need the encouragement of Christian friends, the life-changing power of prayer, and the healing truth of God's Holy Word. If we find ourselves falling into the spiritual traps of worry and discouragement, we should seek the healing touch of Jesus and the encouraging words of fellow Christians. Even though this world can be a place of trials and struggles, God has promised us peace, joy, and eternal life if we give ourselves to Him.

A Heart of Gratitude

I wait for the Lord, my soul waits, and in His word I do hope. My soul waits for the Lord more than those who watch for the morning—yes, more than those who watch for the morning.

Psalm 130:5-6 NKJV

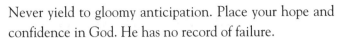

Never yield to gloomy anticipation. Place your hope and confidence in God. He has no record of failure.

Mrs. Charles E. Cowman

The best we can hope for in this life is a knothole peek at the shining realities ahead. Yet a glimpse is enough. It's enough to convince our hearts that whatever sufferings and sorrows currently assail us aren't worthy of comparison to that which waits over the horizon.

Joni Eareckson Tada

I discovered that sorrow was not to be feared but rather endured with hope and expectancy that God would use it to visit and bless my life.

Jill Briscoe

Love is the seed of all hope. It is the enticement to trust, to risk, to try, and to go on.

Gloria Gaither

Today's Prayer

Dear Lord, I will place my hope in You. If I become discouraged, I will turn to You. If I am afraid, I will seek strength in You. In every aspect of my life, I will trust You. You are my Father, and I will place my hope, my trust, and my faith in You. Amen

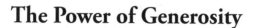

The Power of Generosity

Each person should do as he has decided in his heart—not out of regret or out of necessity, for God loves a cheerful giver.

2 Corinthians 9:7 HCSB

Do you sincerely want to express your gratitude to God? Then make sure that you're a generous woman. When you give generously to those who need your help, God will bless your endeavors and enrich your life. So, if you're looking for a surefire way to improve the quality of your day or your life, here it is: find ways to share your blessings.

God rewards generosity just as surely as He punishes sin. If we become generous disciples in the service of our Lord, God blesses us in ways that we cannot fully understand. But if we allow ourselves to become closefisted and miserly, either with our possessions or with our love, we deprive ourselves of the spiritual abundance that would otherwise be ours.

Do you seek God's abundance and His peace? Then share the blessings that God has given you. Share your possessions, share your faith, share your testimony, and share your love. God expects no less, and He deserves no less. And neither, come to think of it, do your neighbors.

Gratitude for God's Guidance

All goes well for those who are generous, who lend freely and conduct their business fairly.

Psalms 112:5 NLT

All kindness and good deeds, we must keep silent. The result will be an inner reservoir of power.

Catherine Marshall

The measure of a life, after all, is not its duration but its donation.

Corrie ten Boom

As faithful stewards of what we have, ought we not to give earnest thought to our staggering surplus?

Elisabeth Elliot

What is your focus today? Joy comes when it is Jesus first, others second...then you.

Kay Arthur

Today's Prayer

Dear Lord, Your Word tells me that it is more blessed to give than to receive. Make me a faithful steward of the gifts You have given me, and let me share those gifts generously with others, today and every day that I live. Amen

Finding the Right Path

Then He said to them all, "If anyone wants to come with Me, he must deny himself, take up his cross daily, and follow Me."

Luke 9:23 HCSB

When we genuinely turn our hearts toward the face of God, we feel the sense that He is inviting us to walk with Him. And that's precisely the path that we must follow.

Oswald Chambers, the author of the Christian classic devotional text, *My Utmost for His Highest*, advised, "Never support an experience which does not have God as its source, and faith in God as its result." These words serve as a powerful reminder that, as Christians, we are called to walk with God and to obey His commandments. But, we live in a world that presents us with countless temptations to stray far from God's path.

When we behave ourselves as obedient servants, we honor the Father and the Son. When we live righteously and according to God's commandments, He blesses us in ways that we cannot fully understand. So, as this day unfolds, take every step of your journey with God as your traveling companion. Study His Holy Word. Follow His commandments. Support only those activities that further God's kingdom and your spiritual growth. Be an example of righteous living to your friends, to your neighbors, and to your children. Then, reap the blessings that God has promised to all those who accept His invitation of life abundant and life eternal.

A Heart of Gratitude

The LORD says, "I will guide you along the best pathway for your life. I will advise you and watch over you."

Psalm 32:8 NLT

Walk in the daylight of God's will because then you will be safe; you will not stumble.

Anne Graham Lotz

It is a joy that God never abandons His children. He guides faithfully all who listen to His directions.

Corrie ten Boom

Today's Prayer

Lord, sometimes life is difficult. But even when I can't see any hope for the future, You are always with me. And, I can live courageously because I know that You are leading me to a place where I can accomplish Your kingdom's work . . . and where You lead, I will follow. Amen

Big Plans

We know that all things work together for the good of those who love God: those who are called according to His purpose.

Romans 8:28 HCSB

God has big plans for your life, but He won't force His plans upon you. Your Creator has given you the ability to make decisions on your own. With that freedom comes the responsibility of living with the consequences of your choices.

If you seek to live in accordance with God's plan for your life, you will study His Word, you will be attentive to His instructions, and you will be watchful for His signs. You will associate with fellow believers who, by their words and actions, will encourage your own spiritual growth. You will assiduously avoid those two terrible temptations: the temptation to sin and the temptation to squander time. And finally, you will listen carefully, even reverently, to the conscience that God has placed in your heart.

God has glorious plans for your day and your life. So as you go about your daily activities, keep your eyes and ears open . . . as well as your heart.

Gratitude for God's Guidance

Teach me to do Your will, for You are my God. May Your gracious Spirit lead me on level ground.

Psalm 143:10 HCSB

God has plans—not problems—for our lives. Before she died in the concentration camp in Ravensbruck, my sister Betsie said to me, "Corrie, your whole life has been a training for the work you are doing here in prison—and for the work you will do afterward."

Corrie ten Boom

Let's never forget that some of God's greatest mercies are His refusals. He says no in order that He may, in some way we cannot imagine, say yes. All His ways with us are merciful. His meaning is always love.

Elisabeth Elliot

God cannot lead the individual who is not willing to give Him a blank check with his life.

Catherine Marshall

All God's plans have the mark of the cross on them, and all His plans have death to self in them.

E. M. Bounds

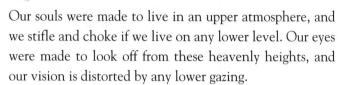

Our souls were made to live in an upper atmosphere, and we stifle and choke if we live on any lower level. Our eyes were made to look off from these heavenly heights, and our vision is distorted by any lower gazing.

Hannah Whitall Smith

God has His reasons. He has His purposes. Ours is an intentional God, brimming over with motive and mission. He never does things capriciously or decides with the flip of a coin.

Joni Eareckson Tada

Every experience God gives us, every person he brings into our lives, is the perfect preparation for the future that only he can see.

Corrie ten Boom

Today's Prayer

Dear Lord, I am Your creation, and You created me for a reason. Give me the wisdom to follow Your direction for my life's journey. Let me do Your work here on earth by seeking Your will and living it, knowing that when I trust in You, Father, I am eternally blessed. Amen

Beyond Worry

Don't worry about anything, but in everything, through prayer and petition with thanksgiving, let your requests be made known to God.

Philippians 4:6 HCSB

I f you are like most women, it is simply a fact of life: from time to time, you worry. You worry about health, about finances, about safety, about relationships, about family, and about countless other challenges of life, some great and some small. Where is the best place to take your worries? Take them to God. Take your troubles to Him, and your fears, and your sorrows.

Barbara Johnson correctly observed, "Worry is the senseless process of cluttering up tomorrow's opportunities with leftover problems from today." So if you'd like to make the most out of this day (and every one hereafter), turn your worries over to a Power greater than yourself . . . and spend your valuable time and energy solving the problems you can fix . . . while trusting God to do the rest.

A Heart of Gratitude

Give your worries to the Lord, and he will take care of you. He will never let good people down.

Psalm 55:22 NCV

Worry is the senseless process
of cluttering up tomorrow's
opportunities with leftover
problems from today.

—

Barbara Johnson

Today is mine. Tomorrow is none of my business. If I peer anxiously into the fog of the future, I will strain my spiritual eyes so that I will not see clearly what is required of me now.

Elisabeth Elliott

Worries carry responsibilities that belong to God, not to you. Worry does not enable us to escape evil; it makes us unfit to cope with it when it comes.

Corrie ten Boom

Are you serious about wanting God's guidance to become the person he wants you to be? The first step is to tell God that you know you can't manage your own life; that you need his help.

Catherine Marshall

The beginning of anxiety is the end of faith, and the beginning of true faith is the end of anxiety.

George Mueller

Today's Prayer

Dear Lord, wherever I find myself, let me celebrate more and worry less. When my faith begins to waver, help me to trust You more. Then, with praise on my lips and the love of Your Son in my heart, let me live courageously, faithfully, prayerfully, and thankfully this day and every day. Amen

Awareness of Your Blessings

Therefore, get your minds ready for action, being self-disciplined, and set your hope completely on the grace to be brought to you at the revelation of Jesus Christ.

1 Peter 1:13 HCSB

Psalm 145 makes this promise: "The LORD is gracious and compassionate, slow to anger and rich in love. The LORD is good to all; he has compassion on all he has made" (vv. 8-9 NIV). As God's children, we are blessed beyond measure, but sometimes, as busy women in a demanding world, we are slow to count our gifts and even slower to give thanks to the Giver. Our blessings include life and health, family and friends, freedom and possessions—for starters. And, the gifts we receive from God are multiplied when we share them with others. May we always give thanks to God for our blessings, and may we always demonstrate our gratitude by sharing them.

A Heart of Gratitude

The Lord is gracious and compassionate, slow to anger and great in faithful love. The Lord is good to everyone; His compassion [rests] on all He has made.

Psalm 145:8-9 HCSB

Jesus intended for us to be overwhelmed by the blessings of regular days. He said it was the reason he had come: "I am come that they might have life, and that they might have it more abundantly."

Gloria Gaither

Do we not continually pass by blessings innumerable without notice, and instead fix our eyes on what we feel to be our trials and our losses, and think and talk about these until our whole horizon is filled with them, and we almost begin to think we have no blessings at all?

Hannah Whitall Smith

When you and I are related to Jesus Christ, our strength and wisdom and peace and joy and love and hope may run out, but His life rushes in to keep us filled to the brim. We are showered with blessings, not because of anything we have or have not done, but simply because of Him.

Anne Graham Lotz

Today's Prayer

Lord, let me be a woman who counts her blessings, and let me be Your faithful servant as I give praise to the Giver of all things good. You have richly blessed my life, Lord. Let me, in turn, be a blessing to all those who cross my path, and may the glory be Yours forever. Amen

Trusting God and Finding Balance

Don't burn out; keep yourselves fueled and aflame. Be alert servants of the Master, cheerfully expectant. Don't quit in hard times; pray all the harder.

Romans 12:11-12 MSG

Life is a delicate balancing act, a tightrope walk with over-commitment on one side and under-commitment on the other. And it's up to each of us to walk carefully on that rope, not falling prey to pride (which causes us to attempt too much) or to fear (which causes us to attempt too little).

God's Word promises us the possibility of abundance (John 10:10). And we are far more likely to experience that abundance when we lead balanced lives.

When you allow yourself to take on too many jobs, you simply can't do all of them well. That means that if you allow yourself to become overcommitted, whether at home, at work, at church, or anywhere in between, you're asking for trouble. So you must learn how to say no to the things you don't have the time or the energy to do.

Of course, sometimes, saying no can be tough. Why? Because well-meaning women (like you) genuinely want to help other people out. But if you allow yourself to become overworked, you may begin over-promising and under-serving—and you'll disappoint just about everybody, including yourself.

Are you and your loved ones doing too much—or too little? If so, it's time to have a little chat with God. And if you listen carefully to His instructions, you will strive to achieve a more balanced life, a life that's right for you and your loved ones. When you do, everybody wins.

Gratitude for God's Guidance

So teach us to number our days, that we may gain a heart of wisdom.

Psalm 90:12 NKJV

Let's face it. None of us can do a thousand things to the glory of God. And, in our own vain attempt to do so, we stand the risk of forfeiting a precious thing.

Beth Moore

The moment you wake up each morning, all your wishes and hopes for the day rush at you like wild animals. And the first job each morning consists in shoving it all back; in listening to that other voice, taking that other point of view, letting that other, larger, stronger, quieter life coming flowing in.

C. S. Lewis

45

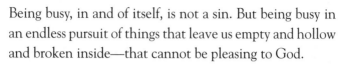

Being busy, in and of itself, is not a sin. But being busy in an endless pursuit of things that leave us empty and hollow and broken inside—that cannot be pleasing to God.

Max Lucado

There is absolutely no evidence that complexity and materialism lead to happiness. On the contrary, there is plenty of evidence that simplicity and spirituality lead to joy, a blessedness that is better than happiness.

Dennis Swanberg

If you've found yourself breathlessly chasing the guy in front of you, break free. Spend some time with your family. Take a walk with someone you love. Hold a three-year-old on your lap and tell him or her a story. Life is simply too short to be spent plodding around in endless circles.

James Dobson

Today's Prayer

I thank You, Father, for Your blessings. Keep me mindful of Your gifts as I find contentment and balance. Let Your priorities be my priorities, and when I have done my best, give me the wisdom to place my faith and my trust in You. Amen

Beyond Envy

Let us walk properly, as in the day, not in revelry and drunkenness, not in lewdness and lust, not in strife and envy.

Romans 13:13 NKJV

In a competitive, cut-throat world, it is easy to become envious of others' success. But it's wrong.

We know intuitively that envy is wrong, but because we are frail, imperfect human beings, we may find ourselves struggling with feelings of envy or resentment, or both. These feelings may be especially forceful when we see other people experience unusually good fortune.

Have you recently felt the pangs of envy creeping into your heart? If so, it's time to focus on the marvelous things that God has done for you and your family. And just as importantly, you must refrain from preoccupying yourself with the blessings that God has chosen to give others.

So here's a surefire formula for a happier, healthier life: Count your own blessings and let your neighbors count theirs. It's the godly way to live.

Gratitude for God's Guidance

Stop your anger! Turn from your rage! Do not envy others—it only leads to harm.

Psalm 37:8 NLT

Discontent dries up the soul.

Elisabeth Elliot

What God asks, does, or requires of others is not my business; it is His.

Kay Arthur

Too many Christians envy the sinners their pleasure and the saints their joy because they don't have either one.

Martin Luther

We might occasionally be able to change our circumstances, but only God can change our hearts.

Beth Moore

The key to contentment is to consider. Consider who you are and be satisfied with that. Consider what you have and be satisfied with that. Consider what God's doing and be satisfied with that.

Luci Swindoll

Today's Prayer

Dear Lord, deliver me from the needless pain of envy. You have given me countless blessings. Let me be thankful for the gifts I have received, and let me never be resentful of the gifts You have given others. Amen

Tackling Tough Times

God is our refuge and strength, a very present help in trouble.

Psalm 46:1 NKJV

Women of every generation have experienced adversity, and this generation is no different. But, today's women face challenges that previous generations could have scarcely imagined. Thankfully, although the world continues to change, God's love remains constant. And, He remains ready to comfort us and strengthen us whenever we turn to Him.

Psalm 147 promises, "He heals the brokenhearted, and binds their wounds" (v. 3). When we are troubled, we must call upon God, and, in His own time and according to His own plan, He will heal us.

If you are like most women, it is simply a fact of life: from time to time, you worry. You worry about health, about finances, about safety, about relationships, about family, and about countless other challenges of life, some great and some small. Where is the best place to take your worries? Take them to God. Take your troubles to Him, and your fears, and your sorrows. Seek protection from the One who cannot be moved.

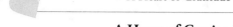

A Heart of Gratitude

God is our refuge and strength, a very present help in trouble.

Psalm 46:1 NKJV

Often the trials we mourn are really gateways into the good things we long for.

Hannah Whitall Smith

Recently I've been learning that life comes down to this: God is in everything. Regardless of what difficulties I am experiencing at the moment, or what things aren't as I would like them to be, I look at the circumstances and say, "Lord, what are you trying to teach me?"

Catherine Marshall

If God sends us on stony paths, he provides strong shoes.

Corrie ten Boom

Today's Prayer

Dear Heavenly Father, when I am troubled, You heal me. When I am afraid, You protect me. When I am discouraged, You lift me up. You are my unending source of strength, Lord; let me turn to You when I am weak. In times of adversity, let me trust Your plan and Your will for my life. And whatever my circumstances, Lord, let me always give the thanks and the glory to You. Amen

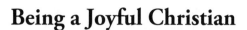

Being a Joyful Christian

Rejoice evermore. Pray without ceasing. In every thing give thanks: for this is the will of God in Christ Jesus concerning you.

1 Thessalonians 5:16-18 KJV

Barbara Johnson says, "You have to look for the joy. Look for the light of God that is hitting your life, and you will find sparkles you didn't know were there."

Have you experienced that kind of joy? Hopefully so, because it's not enough to hear someone else talk about being joyful—you must actually experience that kind of joy in order to understand it.

Should you expect to be a joy-filled woman 24 hours a day, seven days a week, from this moment on? No. But you can (and should) experience pockets of joy frequently—that's the kind of joy-filled life that a woman like you deserves to live.

A Heart of Gratitude

Make me hear joy and gladness.

Psalm 51:8 NKJV

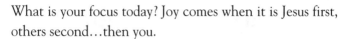

What is your focus today? Joy comes when it is Jesus first, others second…then you.

Kay Arthur

The Christian lifestyle is not one of legalistic do's and don'ts, but one that is positive, attractive, and joyful.

Vonette Bright

If you're a thinking Christian, you will be a joyful Christian.

Marie T. Freeman

There may be no trumpet sound or loud applause when we make a right decision, just a calm sense of resolution and peace.

Gloria Gaither

Jesus did not promise to change the circumstances around us. He promised great peace and pure joy to those who would learn to believe that God actually controls all things.

Corrie ten Boom

Today's Prayer

Dear Lord, You have given me so many blessings, starting with my family. I will keep joy in my heart as I thank You, Lord, for every single blessing You've given me. Amen

Finding Passion

He did it with all his heart. So he prospered.

2 Chronicles 31:21 NKJV

Are you passionate about your life, your loved ones, your work, and your Savior? As a believer who has been saved by a risen Christ, you should be.

Why did Christ endure the humiliation and torture of the cross? He did it for you. His love is as near as your next breath, as personal as your next thought, more essential than your next heartbeat. And what must you do in response to the Savior's gifts? You must accept His love, praise His name, and share His message of salvation. And, you must conduct yourself in a manner that demonstrates to all the world that your acquaintance with the Master is not a passing fancy, but that it is, instead, the cornerstone and the touchstone of your life.

As a thoughtful Christian, you have every reason to be enthusiastic about life, but sometimes the struggles of everyday living may leave you feeling exhausted and discouraged. If your passion for life is slowly fading away, it's time to slow down, to rest, to recount your blessings, to worship, and to pray.

John Wesley advised, "Catch on fire with enthusiasm and people will come for miles to watch you burn." His

53

words still ring true. When you fan the flames of enthusiasm, your faith serves as a beacon to others.

Our world desperately needs faithful believers who are passionate about their lives and their faith. Be such a believer. The world desperately needs your enthusiasm, and just as importantly, you need the experience of sharing it.

When you allow Christ to reign over your heart—when you worship Him with words, thoughts, prayers, and deeds—your life can become a glorious adventure. When you live passionately—and share your passion with others—God will most certainly bless you and yours . . . today and forever.

A Heart of Gratitude

Delight yourself also in the Lord, and He shall give you the desires of your heart.

Psalm 37:4 NKJV

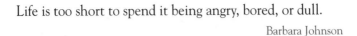

Life is too short to spend it being angry, bored, or dull.

Barbara Johnson

Success or failure can be pretty well predicted by the degree to which the heart is fully in it.

John Eldredge

We honor God by asking for great things when they are part of His promise. We dishonor Him and cheat ourselves when we ask for molehills where He has offered mountains.

Vance Havner

One of the great needs in the church today is for every Christian to become enthusiastic about his faith in Jesus Christ.

Billy Graham

Today's Prayer

Heavenly Father, thank You for the gift of Your Son Jesus. I will be His faithful, obedient servant, and I will make fundamental changes in my life for Him. I will be a passionate believer, and I will praise You for Your blessings, for Your love, and for Your Son. Amen

Following Your Conscience

Let us draw near with a true heart in full assurance of faith, our hearts sprinkled clean from an evil conscience and our bodies washed in pure water.

Hebrews 10:22 HCSB

God gave you a conscience for a very good reason: to make your path conform to His will. Billy Graham correctly observed, "Most of us follow our conscience as we follow a wheelbarrow. We push it in front of us in the direction we want to go." To do so, of course, is a profound mistake. Yet all of us, on occasion, have failed to listen to the voice that God planted in our hearts, and all of us have suffered the consequences.

Wise believers make it a practice to listen carefully to that quiet internal voice. Count yourself among that number. When your conscience speaks, listen and learn. In all likelihood, God is trying to get His message through. And in all likelihood, it is a message that you desperately need to hear.

Gratitude for God's Guidance

Blessed is every one who fears the Lord, who walks in His ways.

Psalm 128:1 NKJV

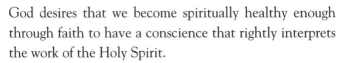
God desires that we become spiritually healthy enough through faith to have a conscience that rightly interprets the work of the Holy Spirit.

Beth Moore

If I am walking along the street with a very disfiguring hole in the back of my dress, of which I am in ignorance, it is certainly a very great comfort to me to have a kind friend who will tell me of it. And similarly, it is indeed a comfort to know that there is always abiding with me a divine, all-seeing Comforter, who will reprove me for all my faults and will not let me go on in a fatal unconsciousness of them.

Hannah Whitall Smith

My conscience is captive to the word of God.

Martin Luther

There is no pillow so soft as a clear conscience.

Old Saying

Today's Prayer

Dear Lord, You speak to me through the Bible, through teachers, and through friends. And, Father, You speak to me through that still, small voice that warns me when I stray from Your will. In these quiet moments and throughout the day, show me Your plan for my life, Lord, that I might serve You. Amen

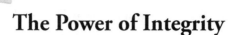

The Power of Integrity

A good name is to be chosen over great wealth.

Proverbs 22:1 HCSB

Honesty is the best policy, but it is not always the easiest policy. Sometimes, the truth hurts, and sometimes, it's tough to be a woman of integrity . . . tough, but essential.

Charles Swindoll correctly observed, "Nothing speaks louder or more powerfully than a life of integrity." Godly women agree.

Integrity is built slowly over a lifetime. It is the sum of every right decision and every honest word. It is forged on the anvil of honorable work and polished by the twin virtues of honesty and fairness. Integrity is a precious thing—difficult to build but easy to tear down. As believers in Christ, we must seek to live each day with discipline, honesty, and faith. When we do, integrity becomes a habit. And God smiles.

Gratitude for God's Guidance

The righteous thrive like a palm tree and grow like a cedar tree in Lebanon.

Psalm 92:12 HCSB

God never called us to naïveté.
He called us to integrity....
The biblical concept of integrity
emphasizes mature innocence
not childlike ignorance.

—

Beth Moore

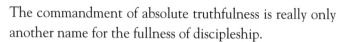
The commandment of absolute truthfulness is really only another name for the fullness of discipleship.

Dietrich Bonhoeffer

Much guilt arises in the life of the believer from practicing the chameleon life of environmental adaptation.

Beth Moore

Maintaining your integrity in a world of sham is no small accomplishment.

Wayne Oates

Integrity is the glue that holds our way of life together. We must constantly strive to keep our integrity intact. When wealth is lost, nothing is lost; when health is lost, something is lost; when character is lost, all is lost.

Billy Graham

Today's Prayer

Dear Lord, You search my heart and know me far better than I know myself. May I be Your worthy servant, and may I live according to Your commandments. Let me be a woman of integrity, Lord, and let my words and deeds be a testimony to You, today and always. Amen

Staying Involved in Your Church

And I also say to you that you are Peter, and on this rock I will build My church, and the forces of Hades will not overpower it. I will give you the keys of the kingdom of heaven, and whatever you bind on earth will have been bound in heaven, and whatever you loose on earth will have been loosed in heaven.

Matthew 16:18-19 HCSB

If you want to build a better life, the church is a wonderful place to do it. Are you an active, contributing, member of your local fellowship? The answer to this simple question will have a profound impact on the direction of your spiritual journey and the content of your character.

If you are not currently engaged in a local church, you're missing out on an array of blessings that include, but are certainly not limited to, the life-lifting relationships that you can—and should—be experiencing with fellow believers.

So do yourself a favor: Find a congregation you're comfortable with, and join it. And once you've joined, don't just attend church out of habit. Go to church out of a sincere desire to know and worship God. When you do, you'll be blessed by the men and women who attend your fellowship, and you'll be blessed by your Creator.

A Heart of Gratitude

Worship the Lord with gladness. Come before him, singing with joy. Acknowledge that the Lord is God! He made us, and we are his. We are his people, the sheep of his pasture.

Psalm 100:2-3 NLT

Our churches are meant to be havens where the caste rules of the world do not apply.

Beth Moore

Be filled with the Holy Spirit; join a church where the members believe the Bible and know the Lord; seek the fellowship of other Christians; learn and be nourished by God's Word and His many promises. Conversion is not the end of your journey—it is only the beginning.

Corrie ten Boom

In God's economy you will be hard-pressed to find many examples of successful "Lone Rangers."

Luci Swindoll

Someone has said that the Church at its very worst is better than the world at its best.

Gloria Gaither

Churches do not lack great scholars and great minds. They lack men and women who can and will be channels of the power of God.

Corrie ten Boom

And how can we improve the church? Simply and only by improving ourselves.

A. W. Tozer

Every time a new person comes to God, every time someone's gifts find expression in the fellowship of believers, every time a family in need is surrounded by the caring church, the truth is affirmed anew: the Church triumphant is alive and well!

Gloria Gaither

Only participation in the full life of a local church builds spiritual muscle.

Rick Warren

Today's Prayer

Dear Lord, today I pray for Your church. Let me help to feed Your flock by helping to build Your church so that others, too, might experience Your enduring love and Your eternal grace. Amen

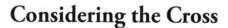

Considering the Cross

But God forbid that I should boast except in the cross of our Lord Jesus Christ, by whom the world has been crucified to me, and I to the world.

Galatians 6:14 NKJV

As we consider Christ's sacrifice on the cross, we should be profoundly humbled and profoundly grateful. And today, as we come to Christ in prayer, we should do so in a spirit of quiet, heartfelt devotion to the One who gave His life so that we might have life eternal.

He was the Son of God, but He wore a crown of thorns. He was the Savior of mankind, yet He was put to death on a roughhewn cross made of wood. He offered His healing touch to an unsaved world, and yet the same hands that had healed the sick and raised the dead were pierced with nails.

Christ humbled Himself on a cross—for you. He shed His blood—for you. He has offered to walk with you through this life and throughout all eternity. As you approach Him today in prayer, think about His sacrifice and His grace. And be humble.

A Heart of Gratitude

Praise the Lord, all you Gentiles! Laud Him, all you peoples! For His merciful kindness is great toward us, and the truth of the Lord endures forever. Praise the Lord!

Psalm 117:1-2 NKJV

God is my Heavenly Father. He loves me with an everlasting love. The proof of that is the Cross.

Elisabeth Elliot

The cross takes care of the past. The cross takes care of the flesh. The cross takes care of the world.

Kay Arthur

God proved his love on the cross. When Christ hung, and bled, and died it was God saying to the world—I love you.

Billy Graham

Today's Prayer

Dear Jesus, You are my Savior and my Protector. You suffered on the cross for me, and I will give You honor and praise every day of my life. I will honor You with my words, my thoughts, and my prayers. And I will live according to Your commandments, so that through me, others might come to know Your perfect love. Amen

65

Do You Believe in Miracles?

For nothing will be impossible with God.

Luke 1:37 HCSB

I f you haven't seen any of God's miracles lately, you haven't been looking. Throughout history, the Creator has intervened in the course of human events in ways that cannot be explained by science or human rationale. And He's still doing so today.

God's miracles are not limited to special occasions, nor are they witnessed by a select few. God is crafting His wonders all around us: the miracle of the birth of a new baby; the miracle of a world renewing itself with every sunrise; the miracle of lives transformed by God's love and grace. Each day, God's handiwork is evident for all to see and experience.

Today, seize the opportunity to inspect God's hand at work. His miracles come in a variety of shapes and sizes, so keep your eyes and your heart open. Be watchful, and you'll soon be amazed.

A Heart of Gratitude

You are the God who works wonders; You revealed Your strength among the peoples.

Psalm 77:14 HCSB

When we face an impossible situation, all self-reliance and self-confidence must melt away; we must be totally dependent on Him for the resources.

Anne Graham Lotz

There is Someone who makes possible what seems completely impossible.

Catherine Marshall

I could go through this day oblivious to the miracles all around me or I could tune in and "enjoy."

Gloria Gaither

Faith means believing in realities that go beyond sense and sight. It is the awareness of unseen divine realities all around you.

Joni Eareckson Tada

Today's Prayer

Dear God, nothing is impossible for You. Your infinite power is beyond human understanding—keep me always mindful of Your strength. When I lose hope, give me faith; when others lose hope, let me tell them of Your glory and Your works. Today, Lord, let me expect the miraculous, and let me trust in You. Amen

Do It Now

When you make a vow to God, don't delay fulfilling it, because He does not delight in fools. Fulfill what you vow.

Ecclesiastes 5:4 HCSB

The old saying is both familiar and true: actions speak louder than words. And as believers, we must beware: our actions should always give credence to the changes that Christ can make in the lives of those who walk with Him.

God calls upon each of us to act in accordance with His will and with respect for His commandments. If we are to be responsible believers, we must realize that it is never enough simply to hear the instructions of God; we must also live by them. And it is never enough to wait idly by while others do God's work here on earth; we, too, must act. Doing God's work is a responsibility that each of us must bear, and when we do, our loving Heavenly Father rewards our efforts with a bountiful harvest.

Gratitude for God's Guidance

People who do what is right may have many problems, but the Lord will solve them all.

Psalm 34:19 NCV

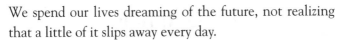

We spend our lives dreaming of the future, not realizing that a little of it slips away every day.

Barbara Johnson

A bird does not know it can fly before it uses its wings. We learn God's love in our hearts as soon as we act upon it.

Corrie ten Boom

From the very moment one feels called to act is born the strength to bear whatever horror one will feel or see. In some inexplicable way, terror loses its overwhelming power when it becomes a task that must be faced.

Emmi Bonhoeffer

God has lots of folks who intend to go to work for him "some day." What He needs is more people who are willing to work for Him this day.

Marie T. Freeman

Today's Prayer

Dear Lord, I have heard Your Word, and I have felt Your presence in my heart; let me act accordingly. Let my words and deeds serve as a testimony to the changes You have made in my life. Let me praise You, Father, by following in the footsteps of Your Son, and let others see Him through me. Amen

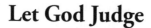

Let God Judge

Do not judge, and you will not be judged. Do not condemn, and you will not be condemned. Forgive, and you will be forgiven.

Luke 6:37 HCSB

We have all fallen short of God's commandments, and He has forgiven us. We, too, must forgive others. And, we must refrain from judging them.

Are you one of those people who finds it easy to judge others? If so, it's time to change.

God does not need (or, for that matter, want) your help. Why? Because God is perfectly capable of judging the human heart . . . while you are not.

As Christians, we are warned that to judge others is to invite fearful consequences: to the extent we judge others, so, too, will we be judged by God. Let us refrain, then, from judging our neighbors. Instead, let us forgive them and love them in the same way that God has forgiven us.

Gratitude for God's Guidance

Speak and act as those who will be judged by the law of freedom. For judgment is without mercy to the one who hasn't shown mercy. Mercy triumphs over judgment.

James 2:12-13 HCSB

Don't judge other people more harshly than you want God to judge you.

Marie T. Freeman

An individual Christian may see fit to give up all sorts of things for special reasons—marriage, or meat, or beer, or cinema; but the moment he starts saying these things are bad in themselves, or looking down his nose at other people who do use them, he has taken the wrong turn.

C. S. Lewis

Christians think they are prosecuting attorneys or judges, when, in reality, God has called all of us to be witnesses.

Warren Wiersbe

No creed or school of thought can monopolize the Spirit of God.

Oswald Chambers

Today's Prayer

Dear Lord, sometimes I am quick to judge others. But, You have commanded me not to judge. Keep me mindful, Father, that when I judge others, I am living outside of Your will for my life. You have forgiven me, Lord. Let me forgive others, let me love them, and let me help them . . . without judging them. Amen

So Many Choices

*But seek first the kingdom of God and His righteousness, and
all these things shall be added to you.*

Matthew 6:33 NKJV

L ife is a series of choices. From the instant we wake
in the morning until the moment we nod off to
sleep at night, we make countless decisions: decisions about the things we do, decisions about the words
we speak, and decisions about the thoughts we choose to
think. Simply put, the quality of those decisions determines the quality of our lives.

As believers who have been saved by a loving and
merciful God, we have every reason to make wise choices.
Yet sometimes, amid the inevitable hustle and bustle of
life here on earth, we allow ourselves to behave in ways
that we know are displeasing to God. When we do, we
forfeit—albeit temporarily—the joy and the peace that we
might otherwise experience through Him.

As you consider the next step in your life's journey,
take time to consider how many things in this life you can
control: your thoughts, your words, your priorities, and
your actions, for starters. And then, if you sincerely want
to discover God's purpose for your life, make choices that
are pleasing to Him. He deserves no less . . . and neither
do you.

Gratitude for God's Guidance

Teach me, O Lord, the way of Your statutes, and I shall keep it to the end. Give me understanding, and I shall keep Your law; indeed, I shall observe it with my whole heart.

Psalm 119:33-34 NKJV

Every day of our lives we make choices about how we're going to live that day.

Luci Swindoll

There may be no trumpet sound or loud applause when we make a right decision, just a calm sense of resolution and peace.

Gloria Gaither

No matter how many books you read, no matter how many schools you attend, you're never really wise until you start making wise choices.

Marie T. Freeman

Today's Prayer

Heavenly Father, I have many choices to make. Help me choose wisely as I follow in the footsteps of Your only begotten Son. Amen

Guard Your Heart

Finally, brethren, whatever things are true, whatever things are noble, whatever things are just, whatever things are pure, whatever things are lovely, whatever things are of good report, if there is any virtue and if there is anything praiseworthy—meditate on these things.

Philippians 4:8 NKJV

You are near and dear to God. He loves you more than you can imagine, and He wants the very best for you. And one more thing: God wants you to guard your heart.

Every day, you are faced with choices . . . more choices than you can count. You can do the right thing, or not. You can be prudent, or not. You can be kind, and generous, and obedient to God. Or not.

Today, the world will offer you countless opportunities to let down your guard and, by doing so, make needless mistakes that may injure you or your loved ones. So be watchful and obedient. Guard your heart by giving it to your Heavenly Father; it is safe with Him.

Gratitude for God's Guidance

Teach me to do thy will; for thou art my God: thy Spirit is good; lead me into the land of uprightness.

Psalm 143:10 KJV

Becoming pure is a process of spiritual growth, and taking seriously the confession of sin during prayer time moves that process along, causing us to purge our life of practices that displease God.

Elizabeth George

Holiness has never been the driving force of the majority. It is, however, mandatory for anyone who wants to enter the kingdom.

Elisabeth Elliot

He doesn't need an abundance of words. He doesn't need a dissertation about your life. He just wants your attention. He wants your heart.

Kathy Troccoli

Prayer keeps us in constant communion with God, which is the goal of our entire believing lives.

Beth Moore

Today's Prayer

Dear Lord, I will guard my heart against the evils, the temptations, and the distractions of this world. I will focus, instead, upon Your love, Your blessings, and Your Son. Amen

During Difficult Days

We also have joy with our troubles, because we know that these troubles produce patience. And patience produces character, and character produces hope.

Romans 5:3-4 NCV

All of us face those occasional days when the traffic jams and the dog gobbles the homework. But, when we find ourselves overtaken by the minor frustrations of life, we must catch ourselves, take a deep breath, and lift our thoughts upward. Although we are here on earth struggling to rise above the distractions of the day, we need never struggle alone. God is here—eternally and faithfully, with infinite patience and love—and, if we reach out to Him, He will restore perspective and peace to our souls.

Sometimes even the most devout Christians can become discouraged, and you are no exception. After all, you live in a world where expectations can be high and demands can be even higher.

If you find yourself enduring difficult circumstances, remember that God remains in His heaven. If you become discouraged with the direction of your day or your life, lift your thoughts and prayers to Him. He is a God of possibility, not negativity. He will guide you through your difficulties and beyond them. Then, you can thank the Giver of

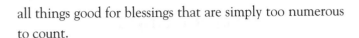

all things good for blessings that are simply too numerous to count.

A Heart of Gratitude

The Lord is a refuge for the oppressed, a refuge in times of trouble.

Psalm 9:9 HCSB

The strengthening of faith comes from staying with it in the hour of trial. We should not shrink from tests of faith.

Catherine Marshall

Our Heavenly Father never takes anything from his children unless he means to give them something better.

George Mueller

Every misfortune, every failure, every loss may be transformed. God has the power to transform all misfortunes into "God-sends."

Mrs. Charles E. Cowman

Today's Prayer

Dear Lord, let my faith be in You, and in You alone. Without You, I am weak, but when I trust You, I am protected. In every aspect of my life, Father, let me place my hope and my trust in Your infinite wisdom and Your boundless grace. Amen

Beyond Anger

Don't let the sun go down on your anger, and don't give the Devil an opportunity.

Ephesians 4:26-27 HCSB

Sometimes, anger is appropriate. Even Jesus became angry when confronted with the moneychangers in the temple. On occasion, you, like Jesus, will confront evil, and when you do, you may respond as He did: vigorously and without reservation. But, more often than not, your frustrations will be of the more mundane variety. As long as you live here on earth, you will face countless opportunities to lose your temper over small, relatively insignificant events: a traffic jam, a spilled cup of coffee, an inconsiderate comment, a broken promise. When you are tempted to lose your temper over the minor inconveniences of life, don't. Turn away from anger, hatred, bitterness, and regret. Turn instead to God.

Gratitude for God's Guidance

Refrain from anger and turn from wrath; do not fret—it leads only to evil.

Psalm 37:8 NIV

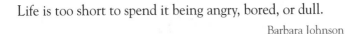
Life is too short to spend it being angry, bored, or dull.

Barbara Johnson

When something robs you of your peace of mind, ask yourself if it is worth the energy you are expending on it. If not, then put it out of your mind in an act of discipline. Every time the thought of "it" returns, refuse it.

Kay Arthur

If your temper gets the best of you . . . then other people get to see the worst in you.

Marie T. Freeman

Anger unresolved will only bring you woe.

Kay Arthur

Anger breeds remorse in the heart, discord in the home, bitterness in the community, and confusion in the state.

Billy Graham

Today's Prayer

Dear Lord, help me to turn away from angry thoughts. Help me always to use Jesus as my guide for life, and let me trust His promises today and forever. Amen

Be Still

In quietness and confidence shall be your strength.

Isaiah 30:15 NKJV

In the first chapter of Mark, we read that in the darkness of the early morning hours, Jesus went to a solitary place and prayed. So, too, should we. But sometimes, finding quiet moments of solitude is difficult indeed.

We live in a noisy world, a world filled with distractions, frustrations, and complications. But if we allow the distractions of a clamorous world to separate us from God's peace, we do ourselves a profound disservice.

If we seek to maintain righteous minds and compassionate hearts, we must take time each day for prayer and for meditation. We must make ourselves still in the presence of our Creator. We must quiet our minds and our hearts so that we can sense God's will, God's love, and God's Son.

Are you one of those busy women who rush through the day with scarcely a single moment for quiet contemplation and prayer? If so, it's time to reorder your priorities.

Has the busy pace of life robbed you of the peace that might otherwise be yours through Jesus Christ? Nothing is more important than the time you spend with your Savior. So be still and claim the inner peace that is your spiritual birthright: the peace of Jesus Christ. It is offered freely; it

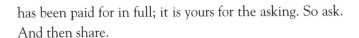
has been paid for in full; it is yours for the asking. So ask. And then share.

Gratitude for God's Guidance

Be still, and know that I am God.

Psalm 46:10 NKJV

The manifold rewards of a serious, consistent prayer life demonstrate clearly that time with our Lord should be our first priority.

Shirley Dobson

The Lord Jesus, available to people much of the time, left them, sometimes a great while before day, to go up to the hills where He could commune in solitude with His Father.

Elisabeth Elliot

Today's Prayer

Lord, Your Holy Word is a light unto the world; let me study it, trust it, and share it with all who cross my path. Let me discover You, Father, in the quiet moments of the day. And, in all that I say and do, help me to be a worthy witness as I share the Good News of Your perfect Son and Your perfect Word. Amen

The Power of Encouragement

Patience and encouragement come from God. And I pray that God will help you all agree with each other the way Christ Jesus wants.

Romans 15:5 NCV

Are you a woman who is a continuing source of encouragement to your family and friends? Hopefully so. After all, one of the reasons that God put you here is to serve and encourage other people—starting with the people who live under your roof.

In his letter to the Ephesians, Paul writes, "Do not let any unwholesome talk come out of your mouths, but only what is helpful for building others up according to their needs, that it may benefit those who listen" (4:29 NIV). This passage reminds us that, as Christians, we are instructed to choose our words carefully so as to build others up through wholesome, honest encouragement. How can we build others up? By celebrating their victories and their accomplishments. As the old saying goes, "When someone does something good, applaud—you'll make two people happy."

Today, look for the good in others and celebrate the good that you find. When you do, you'll be a powerful force of encouragement in your corner of the world . . . and a worthy servant to your God.

A Heart of Gratitude

Be of good courage, and he shall strengthen your heart, all ye that hope in the LORD.

Psalm 31:24 KJV

Always stay connected to people and seek out things that bring you joy. Dream with abandon. Pray confidently.

Barbara Johnson

A single word, if spoken in a friendly spirit, may be sufficient to turn one from dangerous error.

Fanny Crosby

One of the ways God refills us after failure is through the blessing of Christian fellowship. Just experiencing the joy of simple activities shared with other children of God can have a healing effect on us.

Anne Graham Lotz

Today's Prayer

Dear Lord, let me celebrate the accomplishments of others. Make me a source of genuine, lasting encouragement to my family and friends. And let my words and deeds be worthy of Your Son, the One who gives me strength and salvation, this day and for all eternity. Amen

Day 33

Be Disciplined

But I discipline my body and bring it into subjection, lest, when I have preached to others, I myself should become disqualified.

1 Corinthians 9:27 NKJV

Wise women understand the importance of discipline. In Proverbs 28:19, the message is clear: "Those who work their land will have plenty of food, but the ones who chase empty dreams instead will end up poor" (NCV).

If we work diligently and faithfully, we can expect a bountiful harvest. But we must never expect the harvest to precede the labor.

Poet Mary Frances Butts advised, "Build a little fence of trust around today. Fill each space with loving work, and therein stay." And her words still apply.

Thoughtful women understand that God doesn't reward laziness or misbehavior. To the contrary, God expects His children (of all ages) to lead disciplined lives . . . and when they do, He rewards them.

Gratitude for God's Guidance

Teach me your ways, O Lord, that I may live according to your truth! Grant me purity of heart, that I may honor you.

Psalm 86:11 NLT

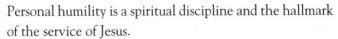
Personal humility is a spiritual discipline and the hallmark of the service of Jesus.

Franklin Graham

True will power and courage are not on the battlefield, but in everyday conquests over our inertia, laziness, and boredom.

D. L. Moody

We set our eyes on the finish line, forgetting the past, and straining toward the mark of spiritual maturity and fruitfulness.

Vonette Bright

God has a present will for your life. It is neither chaotic nor utterly exhausting. In the midst of many good choices vying for your time, He will give you the discernment to recognize what is best.

Beth Moore

Today's Prayer

Dear Lord, make me a woman of discipline and righteousness. Let my conduct show others what it means to be a faithful Christian, and let me follow Your will and Your Word, today and every day. Amen

Accepting God's Calling

But as God has distributed to each one, as the Lord has called each one, so let him walk.

1 Corinthians 7:17 NKJV

God is calling you to follow a specific path that He has chosen for your life. And it is vitally important that you heed that call. Otherwise, your talents and opportunities may go unused.

Have you already heard God's call? And are you pursuing it with vigor? If so, you're both fortunate and wise. But if you have not yet discovered what God intends for you to do with your life, keep searching and keep praying until you discover why the Creator put you here.

Remember: God has important work for you to do—work that no one else on earth can accomplish but you. The Creator has placed you in a particular location, amid particular people, with unique opportunities to serve. And He has given you all the tools you need to succeed. So listen for His voice, watch for His signs, and prepare yourself for the call that is sure to come.

Gratitude for God's Guidance

Teach me to do Your will, for You are my God. May Your gracious Spirit lead me on level ground.

Psalm 143:10 HCSB

God never calls without
enabling us. In other words,
if he calls you to do something,
he makes it possible
for you to do it.

—

Luci Swindoll

With each new experience of letting God be in control, we gain courage and reinforcement for daring to do it again and again.

Gloria Gaither

In the center of a hurricane there is absolute quiet and peace. There is no safer place than in the center of the will of God.

Corrie ten Boom

God never leads us astray. He knows exactly where He's taking us. Our job is to obey.

Charles Swindoll

The God who created and numbers the stars in the heavens also numbers the hairs of my head. He pays attention to very big things and to very small ones. What matters to me matters to Him, and that changes my life.

Elisabeth Elliot

Today's Prayer

Heavenly Father, You have called me, and I acknowledge that calling. In these quiet moments before this busy day unfolds, I come to You. I will study Your Word and seek Your guidance. Give me the wisdom to know Your will for my life and the courage to follow wherever You may lead me, today and forever. Amen

Enthusiasm for Life

Don't work only while being watched, in order to please men, but as slaves of Christ, do God's will from your heart. Render service with a good attitude, as to the Lord and not to men.

Ephesians 6:6-7 HCSB

Do you see each day as a glorious opportunity to serve God and to do His will? Are you enthused about life, or do you struggle through each day giving scarcely a thought to God's blessings? Are you constantly praising God for His gifts, and are you sharing His Good News with the world? And are you excited about the possibilities for service that God has placed before you, whether at home, at work, at church, or at school? You should be.

You are the recipient of Christ's sacrificial love. Accept it enthusiastically and share it fervently. Jesus deserves your enthusiasm; the world deserves it; and you deserve the experience of sharing it.

A Heart of Gratitude

You will teach me how to live a holy life. Being with you will fill me with joy; at your right hand I will find pleasure forever.

Psalm 16:11 NCV

Living life with a consistent
spiritual walk deeply influences
those we love most.

—

Vonette Bright

Your light is the truth of the Gospel message itself as well as your witness as to Who Jesus is and what He has done for you. Don't hide it.

Anne Graham Lotz

Making up a string of excuses is usually harder than doing the work.

Marie T. Freeman

Enthusiasm, like the flu, is contagious—we get it from one another.

Barbara Johnson

To a world that was spiritually dry and populated with parched lives scorched by sin, Jesus was the Living Water who would quench the thirsty soul, saving it from "bondage" and filling it with satisfaction and joy and purpose and meaning.

Anne Graham Lotz

Today's Prayer

Dear Lord, I know that others are watching the way that I live my life. Help me to be an enthusiastic Christian with a faith that is contagious. Amen.

The Right Kind of Fear

Therefore, since we are receiving a kingdom that cannot be shaken, let us hold on to grace. By it, we may serve God acceptably, with reverence and awe.

Hebrews 12:28 HCSB

Are you a woman who possesses a healthy, fearful respect for God's power? Hopefully so. After all, God's Word teaches that the fear of the Lord is the beginning of knowledge (Proverbs 1:7).

When we fear the Creator—and when we honor Him by obeying His commandments—we receive God's approval and His blessings. But, when we ignore Him or disobey Him, we invite disastrous consequences.

God's hand shapes the universe, and it shapes our lives. God maintains absolute sovereignty over His creation, and His power is beyond comprehension. The fear of the Lord is, indeed, the beginning of knowledge. But thankfully, once we possess a healthy, reverent fear of God, we need never be fearful of anything else.

Gratitude for God's Guidance

The fear of the Lord is the beginning of wisdom; a good understanding have all those who do His commandments. His praise endures forever.

Psalm 111:10 NKJV

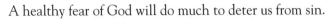

A healthy fear of God will do much to deter us from sin.

Charles Swindoll

The remarkable thing about fearing God is that when you fear God, you fear nothing else, whereas if you do not fear God, you fear everything else.

Oswald Chambers

When true believers are awed by the greatness of God and by the privilege of becoming His children, then they become sincerely motivated, effective evangelists.

Bill Hybels

I'm convinced that there is nothing that can happen to me in this life that is not precisely designed by a sovereign Lord to give me the opportunity to learn to know Him.

Elisabeth Elliot

God is God. He knows what he is doing.

Max Lucado

Today's Prayer

Dear Lord, let my greatest fear be the fear of displeasing You. I will strive, Father, to obey Your commandments and seek Your will this day and every day of my life. Amen

When You Have Doubts

Now if any of you lacks wisdom, he should ask God, who gives to all generously and without criticizing, and it will be given to him. But let him ask in faith without doubting. For the doubter is like the surging sea, driven and tossed by the wind.

James 1:5-6 HCSB

If you've never had any doubts about your faith, then you can stop reading this page now and skip to the next. But if you've ever been plagued by doubts about your faith or your God, keep reading.

Even some of the most faithful Christians are, at times, beset by occasional bouts of discouragement and doubt. But even when we feel far removed from God, God is never far removed from us. He is always with us, always willing to calm the storms of life—always willing to replace our doubts with comfort and assurance.

Whenever you're plagued by doubts, that's precisely the moment you should seek God's presence by genuinely seeking to establish a deeper, more meaningful relationship with His Son. Then you may rest assured that in time, God will calm your fears, answer your prayers, and restore your confidence.

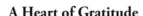

A Heart of Gratitude

When doubts filled my mind, your comfort gave me renewed hope and cheer.

Psalm 94:19 NLT

We are most vulnerable to the piercing winds of doubt when we distance ourselves from the mission and fellowship to which Christ has called us.

Joni Eareckson Tada

Disobedience to His Word will cause you to doubt.

Anne Graham Lotz

Fear and doubt are conquered by a faith that rejoices. And faith can rejoice because the promises of God are as certain as God Himself.

Kay Arthur

Today's Prayer

Dear God, sometimes this world can be a puzzling place, filled with uncertainty and doubt. When I am unsure of my next step, keep me mindful that You are always near and that You can overcome any challenge. Give me faith, Father, and let me remember always that with Your love and Your power, I can live courageously and faithfully today and every day. Amen

God's Love

Dear friends, if God loved us in this way, we also must love one another.

1 John 4:11 HCSB

Because God's power is limitless, it is far beyond the comprehension of mortal minds. But even though we cannot fully understand the heart of God, we can be open to God's love.

God's ability to love is not burdened by temporal boundaries or by earthly limitations. The love that flows from the heart of God is infinite—and today presents yet another opportunity to celebrate that love.

You are a glorious creation, a unique individual, a beautiful example of God's handiwork. God's love for you is limitless. Accept that love, acknowledge it, and be grateful.

A Heart of Gratitude

For the Lord is good, and His love is eternal; His faithfulness endures through all generations.

Psalm 100:5 HCSB

Snuggle in God's arms.
When you are hurting,
when you feel lonely or left out,
let Him cradle you, comfort you,
reassure you of His all-sufficient
power and love.

—

Kay Arthur

Being loved by Him whose opinion matters most gives us the security to risk loving, too—even loving ourselves.

Gloria Gaither

There is no pit so deep that God's love is not deeper still.

Corrie ten Boom

Love is not something God does; love is something God is.

Beth Moore

I love Him because He first loved me, and He still does love me, and He will love me forever and ever.

Bill Bright

The hope we have in Jesus is the anchor for the soul— something sure and steadfast, preventing drifting or giving way, lowered to the depth of God's love.

Franklin Graham

Today's Prayer

Dear God, You are love. You love me, Father, and I love You. As I love You more, Lord, I am also able to love my family and friends more. I will be Your loving servant, Heavenly Father, today and throughout eternity. Amen

Trust God's Promises

For you need endurance, so that after you have done God's will, you may receive what was promised.

Hebrews 10:36 HCSB

What do you expect from the day ahead? Are you expecting God to do wonderful things, or are you living beneath a cloud of apprehension and doubt? The familiar words of Psalm 118:24 remind us of a profound yet simple truth: "This is the day which the LORD hath made; we will rejoice and be glad in it" (KJV).

For Christian believers, every day begins and ends with God's Son and God's promises. When we accept Christ into our hearts, God promises us the opportunity for earthly peace and spiritual abundance. But more importantly, God promises us the priceless gift of eternal life.

As we face the inevitable challenges of life here on earth, we must arm ourselves with the promises of God's Holy Word. When we do, we can expect the best, not only for the day ahead, but also for all eternity.

A Heart of Gratitude

God is faithful, by whom you were called into the fellowship of His Son, Jesus Christ our Lord.

1 Corinthians 1:9 NKJV

God will never let you sink
under your circumstances.
He always provides a safety net
and His love always encircles.

—

Barbara Johnson

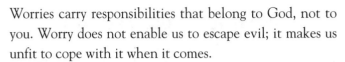
Worries carry responsibilities that belong to God, not to you. Worry does not enable us to escape evil; it makes us unfit to cope with it when it comes.

Corrie ten Boom

A God wise enough to create me and the world I live in is wise enough to watch out for me.

Philip Yancey

The promises of Scripture are not mere pious hopes or sanctified guesses. They are more than sentimental words to be printed on decorated cards for Sunday School children. They are eternal verities. They are true. There is no perhaps about them.

Peter Marshall

God's promises are medicine for the broken heart. Let Him comfort you. And, after He has comforted you, try to share that comfort with somebody else. It will do both of you good.

Warren Wiersbe

Today's Prayer

Lord, Your Holy Word contains promises, and I will trust them. I will use the Bible as my guide, and I will trust You, Lord, to speak to me through Your Holy Spirit and through Your Holy Word, this day and forever. Amen

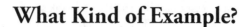

What Kind of Example?

Be an example to the believers in word, in conduct, in love, in spirit, in faith, in purity.

1 Timothy 4:12 NKJV

Whether we like it or not, all of us are role models. Our friends and family members watch our actions and, as followers of Christ, we are obliged to act accordingly.

What kind of example are you? Are you the kind of woman whose life serves as a genuine example of righteousness? Are you a woman whose behavior serves as a positive role model for young people? Are you the kind of woman whose actions, day in and day out, are based upon kindness, faithfulness, and a love for the Lord? If so, you are not only blessed by God, but you are also a powerful force for good in a world that desperately needs positive influences such as yours.

Corrie ten Boom advised, "Don't worry about what you do not understand. Worry about what you do understand in the Bible but do not live by." And that's sound advice because our families and friends are watching . . . and so, for that matter, is God.

Gratitude for God's Guidance

Blessed are they who maintain justice, who constantly do what is right.

Psalm 106:3 NIV

Your light is the truth of the Gospel message itself as well as your witness as to Who Jesus is and what He has done for you. Don't hide it.

Anne Graham Lotz

Living life with a consistent spiritual walk deeply influences those we love most.

Vonette Bright

In your desire to share the gospel, you may be the only Jesus someone else will ever meet. Be real and be involved with people.

Barbara Johnson

Today's Prayer

Dear Lord, help me be a worthy example to my friends and to my family. Let the things that I say and the things that I do show everyone what it means to be a follower of Your Son. Amen

Beyond Bitterness

Hatred stirs up conflicts, but love covers all offenses.

Proverbs 10:12 HCSB

Are you mired in the quicksand of bitterness or regret? If so, it's time to free yourself from the mire. The world holds few if any rewards for those who remain angrily focused upon the past. Still, the act of forgiveness is difficult for all but the most saintly men and women.

Being frail, fallible, imperfect human beings, most of us are quick to anger, quick to blame, slow to forgive, and even slower to forget. Yet we know that it's best to forgive others, just as we, too, have been forgiven.

If there exists even one person—including yourself—against whom you still harbor bitter feelings, it's time to forgive and move on. Bitterness, and regret are not part of God's plan for you, but God won't force you to forgive others. It's a job that only you can finish, and the sooner you finish it, the better.

Gratitude for God's Guidance

Refrain from anger and give up [your] rage; do not be agitated— it can only bring harm.

Psalm 37:8 HCSB

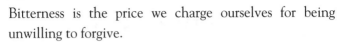

Bitterness is the price we charge ourselves for being unwilling to forgive.

Marie T. Freeman

Forgiveness is the key that unlocks the door of resentment and the handcuffs of hate. It is a power that breaks the chains of bitterness and the shackles of selfishness.

Corrie ten Boom

Bitterness is a spiritual cancer, a rapidly growing malignancy that can consume your life. Bitterness cannot be ignored but must be healed at the very core, and only Christ can heal bitterness.

Beth Moore

Sin is any deed or memory that hampers or binds human personality.

Catherine Marshall

Today's Prayer

Heavenly Father, free me from anger and bitterness. When I am angry, I cannot feel the peace that You intend for my life. When I am bitter, I cannot sense Your presence. Keep me mindful that forgiveness is Your commandment. Let me turn away from bitterness and instead claim the spiritual abundance that You offer through the gift of Your Son. Amen

Serve Him

Be strong and of good courage, and do it; do not fear nor be dismayed, for the Lord God—my God—will be with you. He will not leave you nor forsake you, until you have finished all the work for the service of the house of the Lord.

1 Chronicles 28:20 NKJV

Jesus teaches that the most esteemed men and women are not the self-congratulatory leaders of society but are instead the humblest of servants. But, as weak human beings, we sometimes fall short as we seek to puff ourselves up and glorify our own accomplishments. To do so is wrong.

Today, you may feel the temptation to build yourself up in the eyes of your neighbors. Resist that temptation. Instead, serve your neighbors quietly and without fanfare. Find a need and fill it . . . humbly. Lend a helping hand and share a word of kindness…anonymously. This is God's way.

As a humble servant, you will glorify yourself, not before men, but before God, and that's what God intends. After all, earthly glory is fleeting: here today and all too soon gone. But, heavenly glory endures throughout eternity. So, the choice is yours: Either you can lift yourself up here on earth and be humbled in heaven, or vice versa. Choose vice versa.

A Heart of Gratitude

Serve the Lord with gladness.

Psalm 100:2 HCSB

God wants us to serve Him with a willing spirit, one that would choose no other way.

Beth Moore

In the very place where God has put us, whatever its limitations, whatever kind of work it may be, we may indeed serve the Lord Christ.

Elisabeth Elliot

Through our service to others, God wants to influence our world for Him.

Vonette Bright

So many times we say that we can't serve God because we aren't whatever is needed. We're not talented enough or smart enough or whatever. But if you are in covenant with Jesus Christ, He is responsible for covering your weaknesses, for being your strength. He will give you His abilities for your disabilities!

Kay Arthur

If you want to discover your spiritual gifts, start obeying God. As you serve Him, you will find that He has given you the gifts that are necessary to follow through in obedience.

Anne Graham Lotz

Doing something positive toward another person is a practical approach to feeling good about yourself.

Barbara Johnson

If you love God enough to ask Him what you can do for Him, then your relationship is growing deep.

Stormie Omartian

Have thy tools ready; God will find thee work.

Charles Kingsley

Today's Prayer

Dear Lord, in weak moments, we may try to build ourselves up by placing ourselves ahead of others. But You want us to be humble servants to those who need our encouragement, our help, and our love. Today, we will do our best to follow in the footsteps of Your Son Jesus by serving others humbly, faithfully, and lovingly. Amen

Open Your Heart to God

We know that all things work together for the good of those who love God: those who are called according to His purpose.

Romans 8:28 HCSB

C. S. Lewis observed, "A man's spiritual health is exactly proportional to his love for God." If we are to enjoy the spiritual health that God intends for us, we must praise Him, we must love Him, and we must obey Him.

When we worship God faithfully and obediently, we invite His love into our hearts. When we truly worship God, we allow Him to rule over our days and our lives. In turn, we grow to love God even more deeply as we sense His love for us.

St. Augustine wrote, "I love you, Lord, not doubtingly, but with absolute certainty. Your Word beat upon my heart until I fell in love with you, and now the universe and everything in it tells me to love you."

Today, open your heart to the Father. And let your obedience be a fitting response to His never-ending love.

A Heart of Gratitude

I love the LORD, for he heard my voice; he heard my cry for mercy.

Psalm 116:1 NIV

Loving Him means
the thankful acceptance
of all things that His love
has appointed.

—

Elisabeth Elliot

When an honest soul can get still before the living Christ, we can still hear Him say simply and clearly, "Love the Lord your God with all your heart and with all your soul and with all your mind…and love one another as I have loved you."

Gloria Gaither

Telling the Lord how much you love Him and why is what praise and worship are all about.

Lisa Whelchel

Whatever you love most, be it sports, pleasure, business or God, that is your god.

Billy Graham

Christian love, either towards God or towards man, is an affair of the will.

C. S. Lewis

Today's Prayer

Dear Heavenly Father, You have blessed me with a love that is infinite and eternal. Let me love You, Lord, more and more each day. Make me a loving servant, Father, today and throughout eternity. And, let me show my love for You by sharing Your message and Your love with others. Amen

Studying His Word

*Like newborn infants, desire the unadulterated spiritual milk,
so that you may grow by it in your salvation.*

1 Peter 2:2 HCSB

As a spiritual being, you have the potential to grow in your personal knowledge of the Lord every day that you live. You can do so through prayer, through worship, through an openness to God's Holy Spirit, and through a careful study of God's Holy Word.

Your Bible contains powerful prescriptions for everyday living. If you sincerely seek to walk with God, you should commit yourself to the thoughtful study of His teachings. The Bible can and should be your roadmap for every aspect of your life.

Do you seek to establish a closer relationship with your Heavenly Father? Then study His Word every day, with no exceptions. The Holy Bible is a priceless, one-of-a-kind gift from God. Treat it that way and read it that way.

Gratitude for God's Guidance

The words of the LORD are pure words: as silver tried in a furnace of earth.

Psalm 12:6 KJV

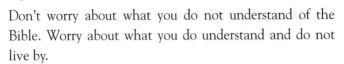
Don't worry about what you do not understand of the Bible. Worry about what you do understand and do not live by.

Corrie ten Boom

The balance of affirmation and discipline, freedom and restraint, encouragement and warning is different for each child and season and generation, yet the absolutes of God's Word are necessary and trustworthy no matter how mercuric the time.

Gloria Gaither

The key to my understanding of the Bible is a personal relationship to Jesus Christ.

Oswald Chambers

The Bible is like no other book. Treat it that way!

Marie T. Freeman

If your Bible is falling apart, chances are your life is staying together.

Anonymous

Today's Prayer

Heavenly Father, Your Holy Word is a light unto my path. In all that I do, help me be a worthy witness for You as I share the Good News of Your perfect Son and Your perfect Word. Amen

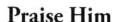

Praise Him

So through Jesus let us always offer to God our sacrifice of praise, coming from lips that speak his name.

Hebrews 13:15 NCV

The words by Fanny Crosby are familiar: "This is my story, this is my song, praising my Savior, all the day long." And, as believers who have been saved by the blood of a risen Christ, we must do exactly as the song instructs: we must praise our Savior many times each day.

Worship and praise must be woven into the fabric of everything we do. Otherwise, we quickly lose perspective as we fall prey to the demands of everyday life.

Do you sincerely seek to be a worthy servant of the One who has given you eternal love and eternal life? Then praise Him for who He is and for what He has done for you. And don't just praise Him on Sunday morning. Praise Him all day long, every day, for as long as you live . . . and then for all eternity.

A Heart of Gratitude

From the rising of the sun to its going down the Lord's name is to be praised.

Psalm 113:3 NKJV

Praise Him! Praise Him! / Tell of His excellent greatness. / Praise Him! Praise Him! / Ever in joyful song!

Fanny Crosby

The time for universal praise is sure to come some day. Let us begin to do our part now.

Hannah Whitall Smith

Praise reestablishes the proper chain of command; we recognize that the King is on the throne and that he has saved his people.

Max Lucado

Nothing we do is more powerful or more life-changing than praising God.

Stormie Omartian

Two wings are necessary to lift our souls toward God: prayer and praise. Prayer asks. Praise accepts the answer.

Mrs. Charles E. Cowman

Today's Prayer

Dear Lord, today and every day I will praise You. I come to You with hope in my heart and words of thanksgiving on my lips. Let me follow in Christ's footsteps, and let my thoughts, my prayers, my words, and my deeds honor You now and forever. Amen

Temptations Everywhere

The good obtain favor from the Lord, but He condemns a man who schemes.

Proverbs 12:2 HCSB

This world is God's creation, and it contains the wonderful fruits of His handiwork. But, the world also contains countless opportunities to stray from God's will. Temptations are everywhere, and the devil, it seems, never takes a day off. Our task, as believers, is to turn away from temptation and to place our lives squarely in the center of God's will.

In his letter to Jewish Christians, Peter offered a stern warning: "Your adversary, the devil, prowls around like a roaring lion, seeking someone to devour" (1 Peter 5:8 NASB). What was true in New Testament times is equally true in our own. Evil is indeed abroad in the world, and Satan continues to sow the seeds of destruction far and wide. As Christians, we must guard our hearts by earnestly wrapping ourselves in the protection of God's Holy Word. When we do, we are protected.

Gratitude for God's Guidance

The face of the Lord is against those who do evil.

Psalm 34:16 NKJV

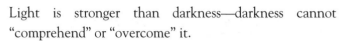
Light is stronger than darkness—darkness cannot "comprehend" or "overcome" it.

Anne Graham Lotz

Where God's ministers are most successful, there the powers of darkness marshal their forces for the conflict.

Lottie Moon

We are in a continual battle with the spiritual forces of evil, but we will triumph when we yield to God's leading and call on His powerful presence in prayer.

Shirley Dobson

We actually are, at present, creatures whose character must be, in some respects, a horror to God, as it is, when we really see it, a horror to ourselves. This I believe to be a fact: and I notice that the holier a man is, the more fully he is aware of that fact.

C. S. Lewis

Today's Prayer

Dear Lord, because You have given Your children free will, the world is a place where evil threatens our lives and our souls. Protect us, Father, from the evils and temptations of this difficult age. Help us to trust You, Father, and to obey Your Word, knowing that Your ultimate victory over evil is both inevitable and complete. Amen

Your Very Bright Future

"For I know the plans I have for you"—[this is] the Lord's declaration—"plans for [your] welfare, not for disaster, to give you a future and a hope."

Jeremiah 29:11 HCSB

How bright is your future? Well, if you're a faithful believer, God's plans for you are so bright that you'd better wear shades. But here's an important question: How bright do you believe your future to be? Are you expecting a terrific tomorrow, or are you dreading a terrible one? The answer you give will have a powerful impact on the way tomorrow turns out.

Do you trust in the ultimate goodness of God's plan for your life? Will you face tomorrow's challenges with optimism and hope? You should. After all, God created you for a very important reason: His reason. And you still have important work to do: His work.

Today, as you live in the present and look to the future, remember that God has an amazing plan for you. Act—and believe—accordingly.

A Heart of Gratitude

Praise the Lord, all nations! Glorify Him, all peoples! For great is His faithful love to us; the Lord's faithfulness endures forever. Hallelujah!

Psalm 117 HCSB

You can look forward with hope, because one day there will be no more separation, no more scars, and no more suffering in My Father's House. It's the home of your dreams!

Anne Graham Lotz

We spend our lives dreaming of the future, not realizing that a little of it slips away every day.

Barbara Johnson

Do not limit the limitless God! With Him, face the future unafraid because you are never alone.

Mrs. Charles E. Cowman

Today's Prayer

Dear Lord, as I look to the future, I will place my trust in You. If I become discouraged, I will turn to You. If I am afraid, I will seek strength in You. You are my Father, and I will place my hope, my trust, and my faith in You. Amen

Asking God

You do not have because you do not ask.

James 4:2 HCSB

God gives the gifts; we, as believers, should accept them—but oftentimes, we don't. Why? Because we fail to trust our Heavenly Father completely, and because we are, at times, surprisingly stubborn. Luke 11 teaches us that God does not withhold spiritual gifts from those who ask. Our obligation, quite simply, is to ask for them.

Are you a woman who asks God to move mountains in your life, or are you expecting Him to stumble over molehills? Whatever the size of your challenges, God is big enough to handle them. Ask for His help today, with faith and with fervor, and then watch in amazement as your mountains begin to move.

Gratitude for God's Guidance

Depend on the Lord and his strength; always go to him for help. Remember the miracles he has done; remember his wonders and his decisions.

Psalm 105:4-5 NCV

When will we realize that we're not troubling God with our questions and concerns? His heart is open to hear us— his touch nearer than our next thought—as if no one in the world existed but us. Our very personal God wants to hear from us personally.

Gigi Graham Tchividjian

God will help us become the people we are meant to be, if only we will ask Him.

Hannah Whitall Smith

Often I have made a request of God with earnest pleadings even backed up with Scripture, only to have Him say "No" because He had something better in store.

Ruth Bell Graham

By asking in Jesus' name, we're making a request not only in His authority, but also for His interests and His benefit.

Shirley Dobson

Today's Prayer

Dear Lord, today I will ask You for the things I need. In every circumstance, in every season of life, I will come to You in prayer. You know the desires of my heart, Lord; grant them, I ask. Yet not my will, Father, but Your will be done. Amen

Lasting Peace

Be of good comfort, be of one mind, live in peace; and the God of love and peace will be with you.

2 Corinthians 13:11 NKJV

Have you found the lasting peace that can—and should—be yours through Jesus Christ? Or are you still chasing the illusion of "peace and happiness" that the world promises but cannot deliver?

The beautiful words of John 14:27 promise that Jesus offers peace, not as the world gives, but as He alone gives: "Peace I leave with you. My peace I give to you. I do not give to you as the world gives. Your heart must not be troubled or fearful" (HCSB). Your challenge is to accept Christ's peace into your heart and then, as best you can, to share His peace with your neighbors. But sometimes, that's easier said than done.

If you are a person with lots of obligations and plenty of responsibilities, it is simply a fact of life: You worry. From time to time, you worry about finances, safety, health, home, family, or about countless other concerns, some great and some small. Where is the best place to take your worries? Take them to God . . . and leave them there.

The Scottish preacher George McDonald observed, "It has been well said that no man ever sank under the burden of the day. It is when tomorrow's burden is added to the burden of today that the weight is more than a man can bear. Never load yourselves so, my friends. If you find yourselves so loaded, at least remember this: it is your own doing, not God's. He begs you to leave the future to Him."

Today, as a gift to yourself, to your family, and to your friends, claim the inner peace that is your spiritual birthright: the peace of Jesus Christ. Christ is standing at the door, waiting patiently for you to invite Him to reign over your heart. His eternal peace is offered freely. Claim it today.

Gratitude for God's Guidance

Those who love your law have great peace and do not stumble.

Psalm 119:165 NLT

The fruit of our placing all things in God's hands is the presence of His abiding peace in our hearts.

Hannah Whitall Smith

Today's Prayer

Dear Lord, the peace that the world offers is fleeting, but You offer a peace that is perfect and eternal. Let me take my concerns and burdens to You, Father, and let me feel the spiritual abundance that You offer through the person of Your Son, the Prince of Peace. Amen

Trusting God's Will

And yet, Lord, you are our Father. We are the clay, and you are the potter. We are all formed by your hand.

Isaiah 64:8 NLT

God has will, and so do we. He gave us the power to make choices for ourselves, and He created a world in which those choices have consequences. The ultimate choice that we face, of course, is what to do about God. We can cast our lot with Him by choosing Jesus Christ as our personal Savior, or not. The choice is ours alone.

We also face thousands of small choices that make up the fabric of daily life. When we align those choices with God's commandments, and when we align our lives with God's will, we receive His abundance, His peace, and His joy. But when we struggle against God's will for our lives, we reap a bitter harvest indeed.

Today, you'll face thousands of small choices; as you do, use God's Word as your guide. And, as you face the ultimate choice, place God's Son and God's will and God's love at the center of your life. You'll discover that God's plan is far grander than any you could have imagined.

Gratitude for God's Protection

God is my shield, saving those whose hearts are true and right.

Psalm 7:10 NLT

Make God's will the focus of your life day by day. If you seek to please Him and Him alone, you'll find yourself satisfied with life.

Kay Arthur

To yield to God means to belong to God, and to belong to God means to have all His infinite power. To belong to God means to have all.

Hannah Whitall Smith

The will of God is never exactly what you expect it to be. It may seem to be much worse, but in the end it's going to be a lot better and a lot bigger.

Elisabeth Elliot

Today's Prayer

Heavenly Father, in these quiet moments before this busy day unfolds, I come to You. I will study Your Word and seek Your guidance. Give me the wisdom to know Your will for my life and the courage to follow wherever You may lead me, today and forever. Amen

The Power of Patience

A patient spirit is better than a proud spirit.

Ecclesiastes 7:8 HCSB

Psalm 37:7 commands us to wait patiently for God. But as busy women in a fast-paced world, many of us find that waiting quietly for God is difficult. Why? Because we are fallible human beings seeking to live according to our own timetables, not God's. In our better moments, we realize that patience is not only a virtue, but it is also a commandment from God.

We human beings are impatient by nature. We know what we want, and we know exactly when we want it: NOW! But, God knows better. He has created a world that unfolds according to His plans, not our own. As believers, we must trust His wisdom and His goodness.

God instructs us to be patient in all things. We must be patient with our families, our friends, and our associates. We must also be patient with our Creator as He unfolds His plan for our lives. And that's as it should be. After all, think how patient God has been with us.

Gratitude for God's Protection

Trust in Him at all times, you people; pour out your heart before Him; God is a refuge for us.

Psalm 62:8 NKJV

Wisdom always waits for
the right time to act,
while emotion always pushes
for action right now.

—

Joyce Meyer

How do you wait upon the Lord? First you must learn to sit at His feet and take time to listen to His words.

Kay Arthur

When we read of the great Biblical leaders, we see that it was not uncommon for God to ask them to wait, not just a day or two, but for years, until God was ready for them to act.

Gloria Gaither

We must learn to wait. There is grace supplied to the one who waits.

Mrs. Charles E. Cowman

As we wait on God, He helps us use the winds of adversity to soar above our problems. As the Bible says, "Those who wait on the LORD…shall mount up with wings like eagles."

Billy Graham

Today's Prayer

Lord, give me patience. When I am hurried, give me peace. When I am frustrated, give me perspective. When I am angry, let me turn my heart to You. Today, let me become a more patient woman, Dear Lord, as I trust in You and in Your master plan for my life. Amen

The Direction of Your Thoughts

Finally brothers, whatever is true, whatever is honorable, whatever is just, whatever is pure, whatever is lovely, whatever is commendable—if there is any moral excellence and if there is any praise—dwell on these things.

Philippians 4:8 HCSB

Thoughts are intensely powerful things. Our thoughts have the power to lift us up or drag us down; they have the power to energize us or deplete us, to inspire us to greater accomplishments, or to make those accomplishments impossible.

Bishop Fulton Sheen correctly observed, "The mind is like a clock that is constantly running down. It needs to be wound up daily with good thoughts." But sometimes, even for the most faithful believers, winding up our intellectual clocks is difficult indeed.

If negative thoughts have left you worried, exhausted, or both, it's time to readjust your thought patterns. Negative thinking is habit-forming; thankfully, so is positive thinking. And it's up to you to train your mind to focus on God's power and your possibilities. Both are far greater than you can imagine.

A Heart of Gratitude

May the words of my mouth and the thoughts of my heart be pleasing to you, O LORD, my rock and my redeemer.

Psalm 19:14 NLT

As we have by faith said no to sin, so we should by faith say yes to God and set our minds on things above, where Christ is seated in the heavenlies.

Vonette Bright

No more imperfect thoughts. No more sad memories. No more ignorance. My redeemed body will have a redeemed mind. Grant me a foretaste of that perfect mind as you mirror your thoughts in me today.

Joni Eareckson Tada

Attitude is the mind's paintbrush; it can color any situation.

Barbara Johnson

It is the thoughts and intents of the heart that shape a person's life.

John Eldredge

Preoccupy my thoughts with your praise beginning today.

Joni Eareckson Tada

The things we think are the things that feed our souls. If we think on pure and lovely things, we shall grow pure and lovely like them; and the converse is equally true.

Hannah Whitall Smith

I became aware of one very important concept I had missed before: my attitude—not my circumstances—was what was making me unhappy.

Vonette Bright

It is the thoughts and intents of the heart that shape a person's life.

John Eldredge

Today's Prayer

Dear Lord, I will focus on Your love, Your power, Your promises, and Your Son. When I am weak, I will turn to You for strength; when I am worried, I will turn to You for comfort; when I am troubled, I will turn to You for patience and perspective. Help me guard my thoughts, Lord, so that I may honor You this day and forever. Amen

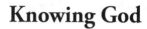

Knowing God

Draw near to God, and He will draw near to you.

James 4:8 HCSB

If you really want to know God, you should start by putting Him first in your life. So here's a question worth thinking about: Have you made God your top priority by offering Him your heart, your soul, your talents, and your time? Or are you in the habit of giving God little more than a few hours on Sunday morning? The answers to these questions will determine, to a surprising extent, the quality of your life and the content of your character.

As you contemplate your own relationship with God, remember this: all of mankind is engaged in the practice of worship. Some folks choose to worship God and, as a result, reap the joy that He offers to His children. Other folks, folks who are stubbornly determined to do it "their way," distance themselves from God by worshiping such things as earthly possessions or personal gratification... and when they do, they suffer.

Does God rule your heart? If you sincerely want to know Him, you must answer yes—you must put your Creator in first place. No exceptions.

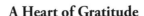

A Heart of Gratitude

My soul thirsts for God, for the living God.

Psalm 42:2 NKJV

Here is our opportunity: we cannot see God, but we can see Christ. Christ was not only the Son of God, but He was the Father. Whatever Christ was, that God is.

Hannah Whitall Smith

You cannot grow spiritually until you have the assurance that Christ is in your life.

Vonette Bright

The only way we can be convinced of Who Jesus is, is through the enlightenment we have received from the Holy Spirit.

Anne Graham Lotz

Today's Prayer

Dear Lord, give me the wisdom to seek You, the patience to wait for You, the insight to hear You, and the courage to obey You, this day and forever. Amen

Your Abundant Life

I have come that they may have life, and that they may have it more abundantly.

John 10:10 NKJV

The familiar words of John 10:10 should serve as a daily reminder: Christ came to this earth so that we might experience His abundance, His love, and His gift of eternal life. But Christ does not force Himself upon us; we must claim His gifts for ourselves.

Every woman knows that some days are so busy and so hurried that abundance seems a distant promise. It is not. Every day, we can claim the spiritual abundance that God promises for our lives…and we should.

Hannah Whitall Smith spoke for believers of every generation when she observed, "God is the giver, and we are the receivers. And His richest gifts are bestowed not upon those who do the greatest things, but upon those who accept His abundance and His grace."

Christ is, indeed, the Giver. Will you accept His gifts today?

Gratitude for God's Guidance

Abundant peace belongs to those who love Your instruction; nothing makes them stumble.

Psalm 119:165 HCSB

The gift of God is eternal life, spiritual life, abundant life through faith in Jesus Christ, the Living Word of God.

Anne Graham Lotz

God's riches are beyond anything we could ask or even dare to imagine! If my life gets gooey and stale, I have no excuse.

Barbara Johnson

It would be wrong to have a "poverty complex," for to think ourselves paupers is to deny either the King's riches or to deny our being His children.

Catherine Marshall

God is the giver, and we are the receivers. And His richest gifts are bestowed not upon those who do the greatest things, but upon those who accept His abundance and His grace.

Hannah Whitall Smith

Today's Prayer

Dear Lord, thank You for the joyful, abundant life that is mine through Christ Jesus. Guide me according to Your will, and help me become a woman whose life is a worthy example to others. Give me courage, Lord, to claim the spiritual riches that You have promised, and show me Your plan for my life, today and forever. Amen

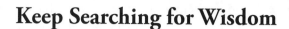

Keep Searching for Wisdom

Now if any of you lacks wisdom, he should ask God, who gives to all generously and without criticizing, and it will be given to him. But let him ask in faith without doubting. For the doubter is like the surging sea, driven and tossed by the wind.

James 1:5-6 HCSB

Where will you find wisdom today? Will you seek it from God or from the world? As a thoughtful woman living in a society that is filled with temptations and distractions, you know that the world's brand of "wisdom" is everywhere . . . and it is dangerous. You live in a world where it's all too easy to stray far from the ultimate source of wisdom: God's Holy Word.

When you commit yourself to the daily study of God's Word—and when you live according to His commandments—you will become wise . . . in time. But don't expect to open your Bible today and be wise tomorrow. Wisdom is not like a mushroom; it does not spring up overnight. It is, instead, like a majestic oak tree that starts as a tiny acorn, grows into a sapling, and eventually reaches up to the sky, tall and strong.

Today and every day, as a way of understanding God's plan for your life, you should study His Word and live by it. When you do, you will accumulate a storehouse of wisdom that will enrich your own life and the lives of your family members, your friends, and the world.

Gratitude for God's Guidance

The Lord says, "I will make you wise and show you where to go. I will guide you and watch over you."

Psalm 32:8 NCV

If we neglect the Bible, we cannot expect to benefit from the wisdom and direction that result from knowing God's Word.

Vonette Bright

"They that sow bountifully shall reap also bountifully," is as true in spiritual things as in material.

Lottie Moon

Today's Prayer

Lord, make me a woman of wisdom and discernment. I seek wisdom, Lord, not as the world gives, but as You give. Lead me in Your ways and teach me from Your Word so that, in time, my wisdom might glorify Your kingdom and Your Son. Amen

Discipleship Now

He has told you men what is good and what it is the Lord requires of you: Only to act justly, to love faithfulness, and to walk humbly with your God.

Micah 6:8 HCSB

When Jesus addressed His disciples, He warned that each one must "take up his cross and follow Me." The disciples must have known exactly what the Master meant. In Jesus' day, prisoners were forced to carry their own crosses to the location where they would be put to death. Thus, Christ's message was clear: in order to follow Him, Christ's disciples must deny themselves and, instead, trust Him completely. Nothing has changed since then.

If we are to be disciples of Christ, we must trust Him and place Him at the very center of our beings. Jesus never comes "next." He is always first. The paradox, of course, is that only by sacrificing ourselves to Him do we gain salvation for ourselves.

Do you seek to be a worthy disciple of Christ? Then pick up His cross today and every day that you live. When you do, He will bless you now and forever.

Gratitude for God's Guidance

Teach me, O LORD, to follow your decrees; then I will keep them to the end. Give me understanding, and I will keep your law and obey it with all my heart.

Psalm 119:33-34 NIV

Jesus challenges you and me to keep our focus daily on the cross of His will if we want to be His disciples.

Anne Graham Lotz

A life lived in God is not lived on the plane of feelings, but of the will.

Elisabeth Elliot

When Jesus put the little child in the midst of His disciples, He did not tell the little child to become like His disciples; He told the disciples to become like the little child.

Ruth Bell Graham

Today's Prayer

Dear Lord, thank You for the gift of Your Son Jesus, my personal Savior. Let me be a worthy disciple of Christ, and let me be ever grateful for His love. I offer my life to You, Lord, so that I might live according to Your commandments and according to Your plan. I will praise You always as I give thanks for Your Son and for Your everlasting love. Amen

Let God Guide the Way

The true children of God are those who let God's Spirit lead them.

Romans 8:14 NCV

The Bible promises that God will guide you if you let Him. Your job, of course, is to let Him. But sometimes, you will be tempted to do otherwise. Sometimes, you'll be tempted to go along with the crowd; other times, you'll be tempted to do things your way, not God's way. When you feel those temptations, resist them.

What will you allow to guide you through the coming day: your own desires (or, for that matter, the desires of your friends)? Or will you allow God to lead the way? The answer should be obvious. You should let God be your guide. When you entrust your life to Him completely and without reservation, God will give you the strength to meet any challenge, the courage to face any trial, and the wisdom to live in His righteousness. So trust Him today and seek His guidance. When you do, your next step will be the right one.

Gratitude for God's Protection

The Lord keeps watch over you as you come and go, both now and forever.

Psalm 121:8 NLT

Are you serious about wanting God's guidance to become a personal reality in your life? The first step is to tell God that you know you can't manage your own life; that you need his help.

Catherine Marshall

God's guidance is even more important than common sense. I can declare that the deepest darkness is outshone by the light of Jesus.

Corrie ten Boom

Is God your spare wheel or your steering wheel?

Anonymous

It's a bit like river rafting with an experienced guide. You may begin to panic when the guide steers you straight into a steep waterfall, especially if another course appears much safer. Yet, after you've emerged from the swirling depths and wiped the spray from your eyes, you see that just beyond the seemingly "safe" route was a series of jagged rocks. Your guide knew what he was doing after all.

Shirley Dobson

Today's Prayer

Lord, You have a plan for my life. Let me discover it and live it. Today, I will seek Your will, knowing that when I trust in You, Dear Father, I am eternally blessed. Amen

Big Dreams

With God's power working in us, God can do much, much more than anything we can ask or imagine.

Ephesians 3:20 NCV

Are you willing to entertain the possibility that God has big plans in store for you? Hopefully so. Yet sometimes, especially if you've recently experienced a life-altering disappointment, you may find it difficult to envision a brighter future for yourself and your family. If so, it's time to reconsider your own capabilities . . . and God's.

Your Heavenly Father created you with unique gifts and untapped talents; your job is to tap them. When you do, you'll begin to feel an increasing sense of confidence in yourself and in your future.

It takes courage to dream big dreams. You will discover that courage when you do three things: accept the past, trust God to handle the future, and make the most of the time He has given you today.

Nothing is too difficult for God, and no dreams are too big for Him—not even yours. So start living—and dreaming—accordingly.

A Heart of Gratitude

You are the God who works wonders; You revealed Your strength among the peoples.

Psalm 77:14 HCSB

The future lies all before us. Shall it only be a slight advance upon what we usually do? Ought it not to be a bound, a leap forward to altitudes of endeavor and success undreamed of before?

Annie Armstrong

Allow your dreams a place in your prayers and plans. God-given dreams can help you move into the future He is preparing for you.

Barbara Johnson

If all things are possible with God, then all things are possible to him who believes in him.

Corrie ten Boom

Today's Prayer

Dear Lord, give me the courage to dream and the faithfulness to trust in Your perfect plan. When I am worried or weary, give me strength for today and hope for tomorrow. Keep me mindful of Your healing power, Your infinite love, and Your eternal salvation. Amen

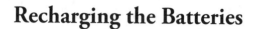

Recharging the Batteries

Finally, brothers, rejoice. Be restored, be encouraged, be of the same mind, be at peace, and the God of love and peace will be with you.

2 Corinthians 13:11 HCSB

Even the most inspired Christians can, from time to time, find themselves running on empty. The demands of daily life can drain us of our strength and rob us of the joy that is rightfully ours in Christ. When we find ourselves tired, discouraged, or worse, there is a source from which we can draw the power needed to recharge our spiritual batteries. That source is God.

God intends that His children lead joyous lives filled with abundance and peace. But sometimes, abundance and peace seem very far away. It is then that we must turn to God for renewal, and when we do, He will restore us.

Are you tired or troubled? Turn your heart toward God in prayer. Are you weak or worried? Take the time—or, more accurately, make the time—to delve deeply into God's Holy Word. Are you spiritually depleted? Call upon fellow believers to support you, and call upon Christ to renew your spirit and your life. When you do, you'll discover that the Creator of the universe stands always ready and always able to create a new sense of wonderment and joy in you.

A Heart of Gratitude

He makes me to lie down in green pastures; He leads me beside the still waters. He restores my soul; He leads me in the paths of righteousness for His name's sake.

Psalm 23:2-3 NKJV

In those desperate times when we feel like we don't have an ounce of strength, He will gently pick up our heads so that our eyes can behold something—something that will keep His hope alive in us.

Kathy Troccoli

God specializes in things fresh and firsthand. His plans for you this year may outshine those of the past. He's prepared to fill your days with reasons to give Him praise.

Joni Eareckson Tada

Today's Prayer

Dear Lord, sometimes the demands of the day leave me discouraged and frustrated. Renew my strength, Father, and give me patience and perspective. Today and every day, let me draw comfort and courage from Your promises, from Your love, and from Your Son. Amen

Too Busy?

Be careful not to forget the Lord.

Deuteronomy 6:12 HCSB

Has the busy pace of life robbed you of the peace that might otherwise be yours through Jesus Christ? If so, you are simply too busy for your own good. Through His Son Jesus, God offers you a peace that passes human understanding, but He won't force His peace upon you; in order to experience it, you must slow down long enough to sense His presence and His love.

Today, as a gift to yourself, to your family, and to the world, slow down and claim the inner peace that is your spiritual birthright: the peace of Jesus Christ. It is offered freely; it has been paid for in full; it is yours for the asking. So ask. And then share.

Gratitude for God's Guidance

In all your ways acknowledge Him, and He shall direct your paths.

Proverbs 3:6 NKJV

In our tense, uptight society where folks are rushing to make appointments they have already missed, a good laugh can be as refreshing as a cup of cold water in the desert.

Barbara Johnson

Frustration is not the will of God. There is time to do anything and everything that God wants us to do.

Elisabeth Elliot

The demand of every day kept me so busy that I subconsciously equated my busyness with commitment to Christ.

Vonette Bright

God is more concerned with the direction of your life than with its speed.

Marie T. Freeman

Today's Prayer

Dear Lord, when the quickening pace of life leaves me with little time for worship or for praise, help me to reorder my priorities. When the demands of the day leave me distracted and discouraged, let me turn to Jesus for the peace that only He can give. And then, when I have accepted the spiritual abundance that is mine through Christ, let me share His message and His love with all who cross my path. Amen

Trust God's Wisdom

Insight is a fountain of life for its possessor, but folly is the instruction of fools.

Proverbs 16:22 HCSB

Where will you place your trust today? Will you trust in the wisdom of fallible men and women, or will you place your faith in God's perfect wisdom? When you decide whom to trust, you will then know how best to respond to the challenges of the coming day.

Are you tired? Discouraged? Fearful? Be comforted and trust God. Are you worried or anxious? Be confident in God's power and trust His Holy Word. Are you confused? Listen to the quiet voice of your Heavenly Father. He is not a God of confusion. Talk with Him; listen to Him; trust Him. He is steadfast, and He is your Protector . . . forever.

Gratitude for God's Guidance

The counsel of the LORD standeth for ever, the thoughts of his heart to all generations.

Psalm 33:11 KJV

We get into trouble when we
think we know what to do
and we stop asking God
if we're doing it.

—

Stormie Omartian

Yielding to the will of God is simply letting His Holy Spirit have His way in our lives.

Shirley Dobson

If you are struggling to make some difficult decisions right now that aren't specifically addressed in the Bible, don't make a choice based on what's right for someone else. You are the Lord's and He will make sure you do what's right.

Lisa Whelchel

Make God's will the focus of your life day by day. If you seek to please Him and Him alone, you'll find yourself satisfied with life.

Kay Arthur

The will of God is never exactly what you expect it to be. It may seem to be much worse, but in the end it's going to be a lot better and a lot bigger.

Elisabeth Elliot

Today's Prayer

Dear Lord, You are my Teacher. Help me to learn from You. And then, let me show others what it means to be a kind, generous, loving Christian. Amen

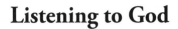

Listening to God

The one who is from God listens to God's words. This is why you don't listen, because you are not from God.

John 8:47 HCSB

Sometimes God speaks loudly and clearly. More often, He speaks in a quiet voice—and if you are wise, you will be listening carefully when He does. To do so, you must carve out quiet moments each day to study His Word and sense His direction.

Can you quiet yourself long enough to listen to your conscience? Are you attuned to the subtle guidance of your intuition? Are you willing to pray sincerely and then to wait quietly for God's response? Hopefully so. Usually God refrains from sending His messages on stone tablets or city billboards. More often, He communicates in subtler ways. If you sincerely desire to hear His voice, you must listen carefully, and you must do so in the silent corners of your quiet, willing heart.

Gratitude for God's Guidance

The Lord says, "I will make you wise and show you where to go. I will guide you and watch over you."

Psalm 32:8 NCV

In the soul-searching of our lives,
we are to stay quiet
so we can hear Him say
all that He wants to say
to us in our hearts.

—

Charles Swindoll

The first service one owes to others in the fellowship consists in listening to them. Just as love of God begins in listening to His Word, so the beginning of love for the brethren is learning to listen to them.

Dietrich Bonhoeffer

The center of power is not to be found in summit meetings or in peace conferences. It is not in Peking or Washington or the United Nations, but rather where a child of God prays in the power of the Spirit for God's will to be done in her life, in her home, and in the world around her.

Ruth Bell Graham

We must leave it to God to answer our prayers in His own wisest way. Sometimes, we are so impatient and think that God does not answer. God always answers! He never fails! Be still. Abide in Him.

Mrs. Charles E. Cowman

Today's Prayer

Lord, give me the wisdom to be a good listener. Help me listen carefully to my family, to my friends, and—most importantly— to You. Amen

The Decision to Celebrate Life

Rejoice in the Lord always. I will say it again: Rejoice!

Philippians 4:4 HCSB

Do you celebrate the gifts God has given you? Do you pray without ceasing? Do you rejoice in the beauty of God's glorious creation? You should. But perhaps, as a busy woman living in a demanding world, you have been slow to count your gifts and even slower to give thanks to the Giver.

As God's children, we are all blessed beyond measure, and we should celebrate His blessings every day that we live. The gifts we receive from God are multiplied when we share them with others. Today is a non-renewable resource—once it's gone, it's gone forever. Our responsibility—as believers—is to give thanks for God's gifts and then use them in the service of God's will and in the service of His people.

God has blessed us beyond measure, and we owe Him everything, including our praise. And let us remember that for those of us who have been saved by God's only begotten Son, every day is a cause for celebration.

A Heart of Gratitude

These things I have spoken to you, that My joy may remain in you, and that your joy may be full.

John 15:11 NKJV

According to Jesus, it is God's will that His children be filled with the joy of life.

Catherine Marshall

If you can forgive the person you were, accept the person you are, and believe in the person you will become, you are headed for joy. So celebrate your life.

Barbara Johnson

Christ is the secret, the source, the substance, the center, and the circumference of all true and lasting gladness.

Mrs. Charles E. Cowman

Today's Prayer

Dear Lord, help us remember that every day is cause for celebration. Today we will try our best to keep joy in our hearts. We will celebrate the life You have given us here on earth and the eternal life that will be ours in heaven. Amen

Praying for Perspective

So if you have been raised with the Messiah, seek what is above, where the Messiah is, seated at the right hand of God.

Colossians 3:1 HCSB

I f a temporary loss of perspective has left you worried, exhausted, or both, it's time to readjust your thought patterns. Negative thoughts are habit-forming; thankfully, so are positive ones. With practice, you can form the habit of focusing on God's priorities and your own possibilities. When you do, you'll soon discover that you will spend less time fretting about your challenges and more time praising God for His gifts.

When you call upon the Lord and prayerfully seek His will, He will give you wisdom and perspective. When you make God's priorities your priorities, He will direct your steps and calm your fears. So today and every day hereafter, pray for a sense of balance and perspective. And remember: no problems are too big for God—and that includes yours.

Gratitude for God's Guidance

We also rejoice in our afflictions, because we know that affliction produces endurance, endurance produces proven character, and proven character produces hope.

Romans 5:3-4 HCSB

Attitude is the mind's paintbrush; it can color any situation.

Barbara Johnson

Like a shadow declining swiftly...away...like the dew of the morning gone with the heat of the day; like the wind in the treetops, like a wave of the sea, so are our lives on earth when seen in light of eternity.

Ruth Bell Graham

Earthly fears are no fears at all. Answer the big questions of eternity, and the little questions of life fall into perspective.

Max Lucado

Instead of being frustrated and overwhelmed by all that is going on in our world, go to the Lord and ask Him to give you His eternal perspective.

Kay Arthur

Today's Prayer

Dear Lord, give me wisdom and perspective. Guide me according to Your plans for my life and according to Your commandments. And keep me mindful, Dear Lord, that Your truth is—and will forever be—the ultimate truth. Amen

Trusting God

Trust in the Lord with all your heart, and do not rely on your own understanding; think about Him in all your ways, and He will guide you on the right paths.

Proverbs 3:5-6 HCSB

When our dreams come true and our plans prove successful, we find it easy to thank our Creator and easy to trust His divine providence. But in times of sorrow or hardship, we may find ourselves questioning God's plans for our lives.

On occasion, you will confront circumstances that trouble you to the very core of your soul. It is during these difficult days that you must find the wisdom and the courage to trust your Heavenly Father despite your circumstances.

Are you a woman who seeks God's blessings for yourself and your family? Then trust Him. Trust Him with your relationships. Trust Him with your priorities. Follow His commandments and pray for His guidance. Trust Your Heavenly Father day by day, moment by moment—in good times and in trying times. Then, wait patiently for God's revelations . . . and prepare yourself for the abundance and peace that will most certainly be yours when you do.

Gratitude for God's Guidance

It is better to trust the Lord than to trust people. It is better to trust the Lord than to trust princes.

Psalm 118:8-9 NCV

Do not be afraid, then, that if you trust, or tell others to trust, the matter will end there. Trust is only the beginning and the continual foundation. When we trust Him, the Lord works, and His work is the important part of the whole matter.

Hannah Whitall Smith

Are you serious about wanting God's guidance to become the person he wants you to be? The first step is to tell God that you know you can't manage your own life; that you need his help.

Catherine Marshall

Today's Prayer

Dear Lord, let my faith be in You, and in You alone. Without You, I am weak, but when I trust You, I am protected. In every aspect of my life, Father, let me place my hope and my trust in Your infinite wisdom and Your boundless grace. Amen

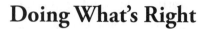

Doing What's Right

For this very reason, make every effort to supplement your faith with goodness, goodness with knowledge, knowledge with self-control, self-control with endurance, endurance with godliness.

2 Peter 1:5-6 HCSB

As Christians, we must do our best to make sure that our actions are accurate reflections of our beliefs. Our theology must be demonstrated, not only by our words but, more importantly, by our actions. In short, we should be practical believers, quick to act whenever we see an opportunity to serve God.

English clergyman Thomas Fuller observed, "He does not believe who does not live according to his beliefs." These words are most certainly true. We may proclaim our beliefs to our hearts' content, but our proclamations will mean nothing—to others or to ourselves—unless we accompany our words with deeds that match. The sermons that we live are far more compelling than the ones we preach.

Like it or not, your life is an accurate reflection of your creed. If this fact gives you cause for concern, don't bother talking about the changes that you intend to make—make them. Your good deeds will speak for themselves.

A Heart of Gratitude

Therefore as you have received Christ Jesus the Lord, walk in Him.

Colossians 2:6 HCSB

We have a decision to make—to turn away from sin or to be miserable and suffer the consequences of continual disobedience.

Vonette Bright

When your good behavior speaks for itself . . . don't interrupt.

Anonymous

Although God causes all things to work together for good for His children, He still holds us accountable for our behavior.

Kay Arthur

There may be no trumpet sound or loud applause when we make a right decision, just a calm sense of resolution and peace.

Gloria Gaither

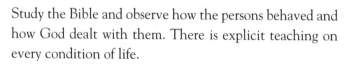
Study the Bible and observe how the persons behaved and how God dealt with them. There is explicit teaching on every condition of life.

Corrie ten Boom

The purity of motive determines the quality of action.

Oswald Chambers

Christians are the citizens of heaven, and while we are on earth, we ought to behave like heaven's citizens.

Warren Wiersbe

Life is a series of choices between the bad, the good, and the best. Everything depends on how we choose.

Vance Havner

Today's Prayer

Dear Lord, this world has countless temptations, distractions, interruptions, and frustrations. When I allow my focus to drift away from You and Your Word, I suffer. But, when I turn my thoughts and my prayers to You, Heavenly Father, You guide my path. Let me discover the right thing to do—and let me do it—this day and every day that I live. Amen

Spiritual Growth

*Like newborn infants, desire the unadulterated spiritual milk,
so that you may grow by it in your salvation.*

1 Peter 2:2 HCSB

When will you be a "fully-grown" Christian woman? Hopefully never—or at least not until you arrive in heaven! As a believer living here on planet earth, you're never "fully grown"; you always have the potential to keep growing.

In those quiet moments when you open your heart to God, the One who made you keeps remaking you. He gives you direction, perspective, wisdom, and courage.

Would you like a time-tested formula for spiritual growth? Here it is: keep studying God's Word, keep obeying His commandments, keep praying (and listening for answers), and keep trying to live in the center of God's will. When you do, you'll never stay stuck for long. You will, instead, be a growing Christian . . . and that's precisely the kind of Christian God wants you to be.

Gratitude for God's Guidance

Therefore, leaving the elementary message about the Messiah, let us go on to maturity.

Hebrews 6:1 HCSB

We set our eyes on the finish line,
forgetting the past, and straining
toward the mark of spiritual
maturity and fruitfulness.

—

Vonette Bright

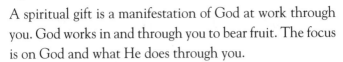

A spiritual gift is a manifestation of God at work through you. God works in and through you to bear fruit. The focus is on God and what He does through you.

Henry Blackaby and Claude King

You are either becoming more like Christ every day or you're becoming less like Him. There is no neutral position in the Lord.

Stormie Omartian

You were born with tremendous potential. When you were born again through faith in Jesus Christ, God added spiritual gifts to your natural talents.

Warren Wiersbe

We should not be upset when unexpected and upsetting things happen. God, in His wisdom, means to make something of us which we have not yet attained, and He is dealing with us accordingly.

J. I. Packer

Today's Prayer

Dear Lord, thank You for the opportunity to walk with Your Son. And, thank You for the opportunity to grow closer to You each day. I thank You for the person I am . . . and for the person I can become. Amen

Gratitude for Your Family

Choose for yourselves today the one you will worship . . . . As for me and my family, we will worship the Lord.

Joshua 24:15 HCSB

As every woman knows, family life is a mixture of conversations, mediations, irritations, deliberations, commiserations, frustrations, negotiations and celebrations. In other words, the life of the typical woman is incredibly varied.

Certainly, in the life of every family, there are moments of frustration and disappointment. Lots of them. But, for those who are lucky enough to live in the presence of a close-knit, caring clan, the rewards far outweigh the frustrations. That's why we pray fervently for our family members, and that's why we love them despite their faults.

No family is perfect, and neither is yours. But, despite the inevitable challenges and occasional hurt feelings of family life, your clan is God's gift to you. That little band of men, women, kids, and babies is a priceless treasure on temporary loan from the Father above. Give thanks to the Giver for the gift of family...and act accordingly.

Gratitude for God's Protection

Unless the Lord builds a house, its builders labor over it in vain; unless the Lord watches over a city, the watchman stays alert in vain.

Psalm 127:1 HSCB

A home is a place where we find direction.

Gigi Graham Tchividjian

Living life with a consistent spiritual walk deeply influences those we love most.

Vonette Bright

Live in the present and make the most of your opportunities to enjoy your family and friends.

Barbara Johnson

Today's Prayer

Dear Lord, I am part of Your family, and I praise You for Your gifts and for Your love. You have also blessed me with my earthly family, and I pray for them, that they might be protected and blessed by You. Let me show love and acceptance for my family, Lord, so that through me, they might come to know and to love You. Amen

Escape from Temptation

The Lord knows how to deliver the godly out of temptations.

2 Peter 2:9 NKJV

If you stop to think about it, the cold, hard evidence is right in front of your eyes: you live in a temptation-filled world. The devil is out on the street, hard at work, causing pain and heartache in more ways than ever before. Here in the 21st century, the bad guys are working around the clock to lead you astray. That's why you must remain vigilant.

In a letter to believers, Peter offered a stern warning: "Your adversary, the devil, prowls around like a roaring lion, seeking someone to devour" (1 Peter 5:8 NASB). What was true in New Testament times is equally true in our own. Satan tempts his prey and then devours them. As believing Christians, we must beware. And, if we seek righteousness in our own lives, we must earnestly wrap ourselves in the protection of God's Holy Word. When we do, we are secure.

Gratitude for God's Protection

Even when I walk through the dark valley of death, I will not be afraid, for you are close beside me. Your rod and your staff protect and comfort me.

Psalm 23:4 NLT

Flee temptation
without leaving
a forwarding address.

—

Barbara Johnson

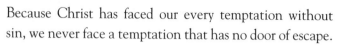
Because Christ has faced our every temptation without sin, we never face a temptation that has no door of escape.

Beth Moore

There is sharp necessity for giving Christ absolute obedience. The devil bids for our complete self-will. To whatever extent we give this self-will the right to be master over our lives, we are, to an extent, giving Satan a toehold.

Catherine Marshall

Lord, what joy to know that Your powers are so much greater than those of the enemy.

Corrie ten Boom

We, as God's people, are not only to stay far away from sin and sinners who would entice us, but we are to be so like our God that we mourn over sin.

Kay Arthur

Today's Prayer

Lord, life is filled with temptations to stray from Your chosen path. Keep me mindful that the life I live and the words I speak bear testimony to my faith. Make me a faithful servant of Your Son, and lead me far from the temptations of this world. Make me a righteous woman, Lord, and let my actions point others to You. Amen

Beyond Fear

Do not fear, for I am with you; do not be afraid, for I am your God. I will strengthen you; I will help you; I will hold on to you with My righteous right hand.

Isaiah 41:10 HCSB

A terrible storm rose quickly on the Sea of Galilee, and the disciples were afraid. Although they had witnessed many miracles, the disciples feared for their lives, so they turned to Jesus, and He calmed the waters and the wind.

Sometimes, we, like Jesus' disciples, feel threatened by the storms of life. When we are fearful, we, too, should turn to Him for comfort and for courage.

The next time you find yourself facing a fear-provoking situation, remember that the One who calmed the wind and the waves is also your Savior. Then ask yourself which is stronger: your faith or your fear. The answer should be obvious. So, when the storm clouds form overhead and you find yourself being tossed on the stormy seas of life, remember this: Wherever you are, God is there, too.

Gratitude for God's Protection

Even when I go through the darkest valley, I fear [no] danger, for You are with me.

Psalm 23:4 HCSB

Worry is a cycle of inefficient
thoughts whirling around
a center of fear.

—

Corrie ten Boom

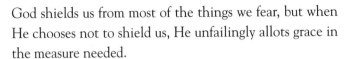
God shields us from most of the things we fear, but when He chooses not to shield us, He unfailingly allots grace in the measure needed.

Elisabeth Elliot

When once we are assured that God is good, then there can be nothing left to fear.

Hannah Whitall Smith

Fear and doubt are conquered by a faith that rejoices. And faith can rejoice because the promises of God are as certain as God Himself.

Kay Arthur

Whether our fear is absolutely realistic or out of proportion in our minds, our greatest refuge is Jesus Christ.

Luci Swindoll

Never be afraid to trust an unknown future to a known God.

Corrie ten Boom

Today's Prayer

Dear Lord, when I am fearful, keep me mindful that You are my protector and my salvation. Thank You, Father, for a perfect love that casts out fear. Because of You, I can live courageously and faithfully this day and every day. Amen

Love According to God

This is My commandment, that you love one another as I have loved you.

John 15:12 NKJV

As a woman, you know the profound love that you hold in your heart for your own family and friends. As a child of God, you can only imagine the infinite love that your Heavenly Father holds for you.

God made you in His own image and gave you salvation through the person of His Son Jesus Christ. And now, precisely because you are a wondrous creation treasured by God, a question presents itself: What will you do in response to the Creator's love? Will you ignore it or embrace it? Will you return it or neglect it? That decision, of course, is yours and yours alone.

When you embrace God's love, your life's purpose is forever changed. When you embrace God's love, you will feel differently about yourself, your neighbors, your family, and your world. More importantly, you will share God's message—and His love—with others.

Your Heavenly Father—a God of infinite love and mercy—is waiting to embrace you with open arms. Accept His love today and forever.

Gratitude for God's Guidance

And may the Lord cause you to increase and overflow with love for one another and for everyone, just as we also do for you.

1 Thessalonians 3:12 HCSB

Those who abandon ship the first time it enters a storm miss the calm beyond. And the rougher the storms weathered together, the deeper and stronger real love grows.

Ruth Bell Graham

Love is an attribute of God. To love others is evidence of a genuine faith.

Kay Arthur

Love is the seed of all hope. It is the enticement to trust, to risk, to try, and to go on.

Gloria Gaither

It is when we come to the Lord in our nothingness, our powerlessness and our helplessness that He then enables us to love in a way which, without Him, would be absolutely impossible.

Elisabeth Elliot

175

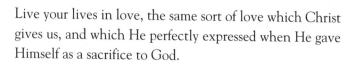

Live your lives in love, the same sort of love which Christ gives us, and which He perfectly expressed when He gave Himself as a sacrifice to God.

Corrie ten Boom

To have fallen in love hints to our hearts that all of earthly life is not hopelessly fallen. Love is the laughter of God.

Beth Moore

If Jesus is the preeminent One in our lives, then we will love each other, submit to each other, and treat one another fairly in the Lord.

Warren Wiersbe

Suppose that I understand the Bible. And, suppose that I am the greatest preacher who ever lived! The Apostle Paul wrote that unless I have love, "I am nothing."

Billy Graham

Today's Prayer

Dear Lord, You have given me the gift of love; let me share that gift with others. And, keep me mindful that the essence of love is not to receive it, but to give it, today and forever. Amen

Look for Fulfillment in All the Right Places

I am the door. If anyone enters by Me, he will be saved, and will come in and go out and find pasture.

John 10:9 HCSB

Where can you find contentment? Is it a result of wealth, or power, or beauty, or fame? Hardly. Genuine contentment springs from a peaceful spirit, a clear conscience, and a loving heart (like yours!).

Our modern world seems preoccupied with the search for happiness. We are bombarded with messages telling us that happiness depends upon the acquisition of material possessions. These messages are false. Enduring peace is not the result of our acquisitions; it is the inevitable result of our dispositions. If we don't find contentment within ourselves, we will never find it outside ourselves.

Thus the search for contentment is an internal quest, an exploration of the heart, mind, and soul. You can find contentment—indeed you will find it—if you simply look in the right places. And the best time to start looking in those places is now.

Gratitude for God's Guidance

How happy are those whose way is blameless, who live according to the law of the Lord! Happy are those who keep His decrees and seek Him with all their heart.

Psalm 119:1-2 HCSB

When we do what is right, we have contentment, peace, and happiness.

Beverly LaHaye

I believe that in every time and place it is within our power to acquiesce in the will of God—and what peace it brings to do so!

Elisabeth Elliot

The circumstances would suggest an utter absence of comfort, yet we find ourselves more than contented.

Lottie Moon

Today's Prayer

Father, let me be a woman who strives to do Your will here on earth, and as I do, let me find contentment and balance. Let me live in the light of Your will and Your priorities for my life, and when I have done my best, Lord, give me the wisdom to place my faith and my trust in You. Amen

Problem-solving 101

Let not your heart be troubled: ye believe in God, believe also in me.

John 14:1 KJV

Face facts: the upcoming day will not be problem-free. In fact, your life can be viewed as an exercise in problem-solving. The question is not whether you will encounter problems; the real question is how you will choose to address them.

When it comes to solving the problems of everyday living, we often know precisely what needs to be done, but we may be slow in doing it—especially if what needs to be done is difficult or uncomfortable. So we put off till tomorrow what should be done today.

The words of Psalm 34 remind us that the Lord solves problems for "people who do what is right" (v. 19 NCV) And usually, doing "what is right" means doing the uncomfortable work of confronting our problems sooner rather than later. So with no further ado, let the problem-solving begin . . . now.

Gratitude for God's Protection

People who do what is right may have many problems, but the Lord will solve them all.

Psalm 34:19 NCV

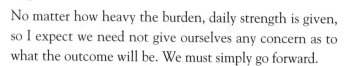
No matter how heavy the burden, daily strength is given, so I expect we need not give ourselves any concern as to what the outcome will be. We must simply go forward.

Annie Armstrong

He that is mastered by Christ is the master of every circumstance. Does the circumstance press hard against you? Do not push it away. It is the Potter's hand.

Mrs. Charles E. Cowman

God helps those who help themselves, but there are times when we are quite incapable of helping ourselves. That's when God stoops down and gathers us in His arms like a mother lifts a sick child, and does for us what we cannot do for ourselves.

Ruth Bell Graham

Today's Prayer

Dear Heavenly Father, when I am troubled, You heal me. When I am afraid, You protect me. When I am discouraged, You lift me up. You are my unending source of strength, Lord; let me turn to You when I am weak. In times of adversity, let me trust Your plan and Your will for my life. And whatever my circumstances, Lord, let me always give the thanks and the glory to You. Amen

Be a Cheerful Christian

A cheerful heart has a continual feast.

Proverbs 15:15 HCSB

On some days, as every woman knows, it's hard to be cheerful. Sometimes, as the demands of the world increase and our energy sags, we feel less like "cheering up" and more like "tearing up." But even in our darkest hours, we can turn to God, and He will give us comfort.

Few things in life are more sad, or, for that matter, more absurd, than a grumpy Christian. Christ promises us lives of abundance and joy, but He does not force His joy upon us. We must claim His joy for ourselves, and when we do, Jesus, in turn, fills our spirits with His power and His love.

How can we receive from Christ the joy that is rightfully ours? By giving Him what is rightfully His: our hearts and our souls.

When we earnestly commit ourselves to the Savior of mankind, and when we place Jesus at the center of our lives and trust Him as our personal Savior, He will transform us, not just for today, but for all eternity. Then we, as God's children, can share Christ's joy and His message with a world that needs both.

A Heart of Gratitude

O clap your hands, all peoples; Shout to God with the voice of joy.

Psalm 47:1 NASB

We may run, walk, stumble, drive, or fly, but let us never lose sight of the reason for the journey, or miss a chance to see a rainbow on the way.

Gloria Gaither

When we bring sunshine into the lives of others, we're warmed by it ourselves. When we spill a little happiness, it splashes on us.

Barbara Johnson

God is good, and heaven is forever. And if those two facts don't cheer you up, nothing will.

Marie T. Freeman

Today's Prayer

Dear Lord, You have given me so many reasons to celebrate. Today, let me choose an attitude of cheerfulness. Let me be a joyful Christian, Lord, quick to smile and slow to anger. And, let me share Your goodness with all whom I meet so that Your love might shine in me and through me. Amen

Choosing to be Kind

And may the Lord make you increase and abound in love to one another and to all.

1 Thessalonians 3:12 NKJV

Christ showed His love for us by willingly sacrificing His own life so that we might have eternal life: "But God demonstrates his own love for us in this: While we were still sinners, Christ died for us" (Romans 5:8 NIV). We, as Christ's followers, are challenged to share His love with kind words on our lips and praise in our hearts.

Just as Christ has been—and will always be—the ultimate friend to His flock, so should we be Christlike in the kindness and generosity that we show toward others, especially those who are most in need.

When we walk each day with Jesus—and obey the commandments found in God's Holy Word—we become worthy ambassadors for Christ. When we share the love of Christ, we share a priceless gift with the world. As His servants, we must do no less.

Gratitude for God's Guidance

Praise the LORD! Oh give thanks to the LORD, for He is good; for His lovingkindness is everlasting.

Psalm 106:1 NASB

Kindness in this world
will do much to help others,
not only to come into the light,
but also to grow in grace
day by day.

—

Fanny Crosby

All kindness and good deeds, we must keep silent. The result will be an inner reservoir of personality power.

Catherine Marshall

A little kindly advice is better than a great deal of scolding.

Fanny Crosby

When we Christians are too busy to care for each other, we're simply too busy for our own good . . . and for God's.

Marie T. Freeman

No matter how crazy or nutty your life has seemed, God can make something strong and good out of it. He can help you grow wide branches for others to use as shelter.

Barbara Johnson

Today's Prayer

Help me, Lord, to see the needs of those around me. Today, let me show courtesy to those who cross my path. Today, let me spread kind words in honor of Your Son. Today, let forgiveness rule my heart. And every day, Lord, let my love for Christ be demonstrated through the acts of kindness that I offer to those who need the healing touch of the Master's hand. Amen

Praying for Guidance

Now if any of you lacks wisdom, he should ask God, who gives to all generously and without criticizing, and it will be given to him. But let him ask in faith without doubting. For the doubter is like the surging sea, driven and tossed by the wind.

James 1:5-6 HCSB

Have you fervently asked God for His guidance in every aspect of your life? If so, then you're continually inviting your Creator to reveal Himself in a variety of ways. As a follower of Christ, you must do no less.

Jesus made it clear to His disciples: they should pray always. So should we. Genuine, heartfelt prayer produces powerful changes in us and in our world. When we lift our hearts to our Father in heaven, we open ourselves to a never-ending source of divine wisdom and infinite love.

Do you have questions about your future that you simply can't answer? Ask for the guidance of your Heavenly Father. Do you sincerely seek to know God's purpose for your life? Then ask Him for direction—and keep asking Him every day that you live. Whatever your need, no matter how great or small, pray about it and never lose hope. God is not just near; He is here, and He's ready to talk with you. Now!

Gratitude for God's Guidance

Show me thy ways, O LORD; teach me thy paths. Lead me in thy truth, and teach me: for thou art the God of my salvation; on thee do I wait all the day.

Psalm 25:4-5 KJV

When there is a matter that requires definite prayer, pray until you believe God and until you can thank Him for His answer.

Hannah Whitall Smith

A prayerful heart and an obedient heart will learn, very slowly and not without sorrow, to stake everything on God Himself.

Elisabeth Elliot

Jesus practiced secret prayer and asked us to follow His example.

Catherine Marshall

Today's Prayer

Dear Lord, I will be a woman of prayer. I will pray about matters great and small. I will bring my concerns to You, Father. I will listen for Your voice, and I will follow in the footsteps of Your Son. Amen

God's Presence

The Lord is with you when you are with Him. If you seek Him, He will be found by you.

2 Chronicles 15:2 HCSB

Since God is everywhere, we are free to sense His presence whenever we take the time to quiet our souls and turn our prayers to Him. But sometimes, amid the incessant demands of everyday life, we turn our thoughts far from God; when we do, we suffer.

Do you set aside quiet moments each day to offer praise to your Creator? As a woman who has received the gift of God's grace, you most certainly should. Silence is a gift that you give to yourself and to God. During these moments of stillness, you will often sense the infinite love and power of your Creator—and He, in turn, will speak directly to your heart.

The familiar words of Psalm 46:10 remind us to "Be still, and know that I am God." When we do so, we encounter the awesome presence of our loving Heavenly Father, and we are comforted in the knowledge that God is not just near. He is here.

Gratitude for God's Protection

I have set the Lord always before me; because He is at my right hand I shall not be moved.

Psalm 16:8 NKJV

It's a crazy world and life speeds by at a blur, yet God is right in the middle of the craziness. And anywhere, at anytime, we may turn to Him, hear His voice, feel His hand, and catch the fragrance of heaven.

Joni Eareckson Tada

In the sanctuary, we discover beauty: the beauty of His presence.

Kay Arthur

Today's Prayer

Heavenly Father, help me to feel Your presence in every situation and every circumstance. You are with me, Lord, in times of celebration and in times of sorrow. You are with me when I am strong and when I am weak. You never leave my side even when it seems to me that You are far away. Today and every day, God, let me feel You and acknowledge Your presence so that others, too, might know You through me. Amen

189

When Mountains Need Moving

I assure you: If anyone says to this mountain, "Be lifted up and thrown into the sea," and does not doubt in his heart, but believes that what he says will happen, it will be done for him.

Mark 11:23 HCSB

Jesus taught His disciples that if they had faith, they could move mountains. You can, too.

When a suffering woman sought healing by merely touching the hem of His cloak, Jesus replied, "Be of good cheer, daughter; your faith has made you well" (Matthew 9:22 NKJV). The message to believers of every generation is clear: we must live by faith today and every day.

When you place your faith, your trust, indeed your life in the hands of Christ Jesus, you'll be amazed at the marvelous things He can do with you and through you. So strengthen your faith through praise, through worship, through Bible study, and through prayer. And trust God's plans. With Him, all things are possible, and He stands ready to open a world of possibilities to you . . . if you have faith.

Gratitude for God's Protection

Cast your burden upon the Lord and He will sustain you: He will never allow the righteous to be shaken.

Psalm 55:22 NASB

Faith is seeing light with the eyes of your heart, when the eyes of your body see only darkness.

Barbara Johnson

Grace calls you to get up, throw off your blanket of helplessness, and to move on through life in faith.

Kay Arthur

Just as our faith strengthens our prayer life, so do our prayers deepen our faith. Let us pray often, starting today, for a deeper, more powerful faith.

Shirley Dobson

Faith does not concern itself with the entire journey. One step is enough.

Mrs. Charles E. Cowman

If God chooses to remain silent, faith is content.

Ruth Bell Graham

Today's Prayer

Dear Lord, help me to be a woman of faith. Help me to remember that You are always near and that You can overcome any challenge. With Your love and Your power, Lord, I can live courageously and faithfully today and every day. Amen

The Wisdom to Be Generous

Freely you have received, freely give.

Matthew 10:8 NKJV

The thread of generosity is woven—completely and inextricably—into the very fabric of Christ's teachings. As He sent His disciples out to heal the sick and spread God's message of salvation, Jesus offered this guiding principle: "Freely you have received, freely give" (Matthew 10:8 NIV). The principle still applies. If we are to be disciples of Christ, we must give freely of our time, our possessions, and our love.

Lisa Whelchel spoke for Christian women everywhere when she observed, "The Lord has abundantly blessed me all of my life. I'm not trying to pay Him back for all of His wonderful gifts; I just realize that He gave them to me to give away." All of us have been blessed, and all of us are called to share those blessings without reservation.

Today, make this pledge and keep it: Be a cheerful, generous, courageous giver. The world needs your help, and you need the spiritual rewards that will be yours when you share your possessions, your talents, and your time.

Gratitude for God's Guidance

So let each one give as he purposes in his heart, not grudgingly or of necessity; for God loves a cheerful giver.

2 Corinthians 9:7 NKJV

When somebody needs a helping hand, he doesn't need it tomorrow or the next day. He needs it now, and that's exactly when you should offer to help. Good deeds, if they are really good, happen sooner rather than later.

Marie T. Freeman

Just pray for a tough hide and a tender heart.

Ruth Bell Graham

What is your focus today? Joy comes when it is Jesus first, others second…then you.

Kay Arthur

We can't do everything, but can we do anything more valuable than invest ourselves in another?

Elisabeth Elliot

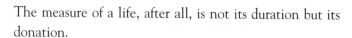

The measure of a life, after all, is not its duration but its donation.

Corrie ten Boom

All kindness and good deeds, we must keep silent. The result will be an inner reservoir of power.

Catherine Marshall

The mind grows by taking in, but the heart grows by giving out.

Warren Wiersbe

Jesus had a loving heart. If he dwells within us, hatred and bitterness will never rule us.

Billy Graham

Today's Prayer

Father, Your gifts are priceless. You gave Your Son Jesus to save us, and Your motivation was love. I pray that the gifts I give to others will come from an overflow of my heart, and that they will echo the great love You have for all of Your children. Amen

Making God's Priorities Your Priorities

Draw near to God, and He will draw near to you.

James 4:8 HCSB

Have you fervently asked God to help prioritize your life? Have you asked Him for guidance and for the courage to do the things that you know need to be done? If so, then you're continually inviting your Creator to reveal Himself in a variety of ways. As a follower of Christ, you must do no less.

When you make God's priorities your priorities, you will receive God's abundance and His peace. When you make God a full partner in every aspect of your life, He will lead you along the proper path: His path. When you allow God to reign over your heart, He will honor you with spiritual blessings that are simply too numerous to count. So, as you plan for the day ahead, make God's will your ultimate priority. When you do, every other priority will have a tendency to fall neatly into place.

Gratitude for God's Protection

Our Lord is great, vast in power; His understanding is infinite.

Psalm 147:5 HCSB

Whatever you love most, be it
sports, pleasure, business or God,
that is your god.

—

Billy Graham

The essence of the Christian life is Jesus: that in all things He might have the preeminence, not that in some things He might have a place.

Franklin Graham

Often our lives are strangled by things that don't ultimately matter.

Grady Nutt

The work of God is appointed. There is always enough time to do the will of God.

Elisabeth Elliot

When we learn to listen to Christ's voice for the details of our daily decisions, we begin to know Him personally.

Catherine Marshall

It's sobering to contemplate how much time, effort, sacrifice, compromise, and attention we give to acquiring and increasing our supply of something that is totally insignificant in eternity.

Anne Graham Lotz

Today's Prayer

Lord, let Your priorities be my priorities. Let Your will be my will. Let Your Word be my guide, and let me grow in faith and in wisdom this day and every day. Amen

Trust Him
When Times Are Tough

Blessed be the God and Father of our Lord Jesus Christ, the Father of mercies and the God of all comfort. He comforts us in all our affliction, so that we may be able to comfort those who are in any kind of affliction, through the comfort we ourselves receive from God.

2 Corinthians 1:3-4 HCSB

The Bible promises this: tough times are temporary but God's love is not—God's love lasts forever. So what does that mean to you? Just this: From time to time, everybody faces tough times, and so will you. And when tough times arrive, God will always stand ready to protect you and heal you.

Psalm 147 promises, "He heals the brokenhearted" (v. 3, NIV), but Psalm 147 doesn't say that He heals them instantly. Usually, it takes time (and maybe even a little help from you) for God to fix things. So if you're facing tough times, face them with God by your side. If you find yourself in any kind of trouble, pray about it and ask God for help. And be patient. God will work things out, just as He has promised, but He will do it in His own way and in His own time.

Gratitude for God's Protection

I will be with you when you pass through the waters . . . when you walk through the fire . . . the flame will not burn you. For I the Lord your God, the Holy One of Israel, and your Savior.

Isaiah 43:2-3 HCSB

Measure the size of the obstacles against the size of God.

Beth Moore

If we're going to stand up and make a difference for Christ while others lounge about, you can be sure we'll encounter hardships, obstacles, nuisances, hassles, and inconveniences—much more than the average couch potato. And we shouldn't be surprised. Such difficulty while serving Christ isn't necessarily suffering—it's status quo.

Joni Eareckson Tada

Adversity is always unexpected and unwelcomed. It is an intruder and a thief, and yet in the hands of God, adversity becomes the means through which His supernatural power is demonstrated.

Charles Stanley

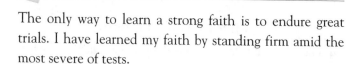
The only way to learn a strong faith is to endure great trials. I have learned my faith by standing firm amid the most severe of tests.

George Mueller

When God allows extraordinary trials for His people, He prepares extraordinary comforts for them.

Corrie ten Boom

When terrible things happen, there are two choices, and only two: We can trust God, or we can defy Him. We believe that God is God, He's still got the whole world in His hands and knows exactly what He's doing, or we must believe that He is not God and that we are at the awful mercy of mere chance.

Elisabeth Elliot

Today's Prayer

Dear Heavenly Father, You are my strength and my protector. When I am troubled, You comfort me. When I am discouraged, You lift me up. When I am afraid, You deliver me. Let me turn to You, Lord, when I am weak. In times of adversity, let me trust Your plan and Your will for my life. Your love is infinite, as is Your wisdom. Whatever my circumstances, Dear Lord, let me always give the praise, and the thanks, and the glory to You. Amen

Beyond Anxiety

Anxiety in a man's heart weighs it down, but a good word cheers it up.

Proverbs 12:25 HCSB

When calamity strikes anywhere in the world, we may be confronted with real-time images, images that breed anxiety. And as we stare transfixed at our television screens, we may fall prey to fear, discouragement, worry, or all three. But our Father in Heaven has other plans. God has promised that we may lead lives of abundance, not anxiety. In fact, His Word instructs us to "be anxious for nothing" (Philippians 4:6). But how can we put our fears to rest? By taking those fears to God and leaving them there.

As you face the challenges of daily life, you may find yourself becoming anxious. If so, turn every one of your concerns over to your Heavenly Father. The same God who created the universe will comfort you if you ask Him...so ask Him and trust Him.

Gratitude for God's Guidance

Don't worry about anything, but in everything, through prayer and petition with thanksgiving, let your requests be made known to God.

Philippians 4:6 HCSB

201

Some people feel guilty about their anxieties and regard them as a defect of faith, but they are afflictions, not sins. Like all afflictions, they are, if we can so take them, our share in the passion of Christ.

C. S. Lewis

So often we pray and then fret anxiously, waiting for God to hurry up and do something. All the while God is waiting for us to calm down, so He can do something through us.

Corrie ten Boom

Worry and anxiety are sand in the machinery of life; faith is the oil.

E. Stanley Jones

We must lay our questions, frustrations, anxieties, and impotence at the feet of God and wait for His answer. And then receiving it, we must live by faith.

Kay Arthur

Today's Prayer

Lord, sometimes this world is a difficult place, and, as a frail human being, I am fearful. When I am worried, restore my faith. When I am anxious, turn my thoughts to You. When I grieve, touch my heart with Your enduring love. Give me the wisdom to trust in You, Father, and give me the courage to live a life of faith, not a life of fear. Amen

God's Timetable

He has made everything appropriate in its time. He has also put eternity in their hearts, but man cannot discover the work God has done from beginning to end.

Ecclesiastes 3:11 HCSB

I f you sincerely seek to be a woman of faith, then you must learn to trust God's timing. You will be sorely tempted, however, to do otherwise. Because you are a fallible human being, you are impatient for things to happen. But, God knows better.

God has created a world that unfolds according to His own timetable, not ours . . . thank goodness! We mortals might make a terrible mess of things. God does not.

God's plan does not always happen in the way that we would like or at the time of our own choosing. Our task—as believing Christians who trust in a benevolent, all-knowing Father—is to wait patiently for God to reveal Himself. And reveal Himself He will. Always. But until God's perfect plan is made known, we must walk in faith and never lose hope. And we must continue to trust Him.

Gratitude for God's Protection

Wait on the LORD; be of good courage, and He shall strengthen your heart; wait, I say, on the LORD!

Psalm 27:14 NKJV

203

We must leave it to God to answer our prayers in His own wisest way. Sometimes, we are so impatient and think that God does not answer. God always answers! He never fails! Be still. Abide in Him.

Mrs. Charles E. Cowman

When we read of the great Biblical leaders, we see that it was not uncommon for God to ask them to wait, not just a day or two, but for years, until God was ready for them to act.

Gloria Gaither

Waiting on God brings us to the journey's end quicker than our feet.

Mrs. Charles E. Cowman

God's silence is in no way indicative of His activity or involvement in our lives. He may be silent, but He is not still.

Charles Swindoll

Today's Prayer

Dear Lord, Your timing is seldom my timing, but Your timing is always right for me. You are my Father, and You have a plan for my life that is grander than I can imagine. When I am impatient, remind me that You are never early or late. You are always on time, Lord, so let me trust in You . . . always. Amen

Letting God Transform Your Life

Your old life is dead. Your new life, which is your real life—even though invisible to spectators—is with Christ in God. He is your life.

Colossians 3:3 MSG

Think, for a moment, about the "old" you, the person you were before you invited Christ to reign over your heart. Now, think about the "new" you, the person you have become since then. Is there a difference between the "old" you and the "new and improved" version? There should be! And that difference should be noticeable not only to you but also to others.

The Bible clearly teaches that when we welcome Christ into our hearts, we become new creations through Him. Our challenge, of course, is to behave ourselves like new creations. When we do, God fills our hearts, He blesses our endeavors, and transforms our lives . . . forever.

Gratitude for God's Guidance

God, create a clean heart for me and renew a steadfast spirit within me.

Psalm 51:10 HCSB

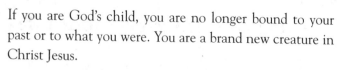
If you are God's child, you are no longer bound to your past or to what you were. You are a brand new creature in Christ Jesus.

Kay Arthur

There is so much Heaven around us now if we have eyes for it, because eternity starts when we give ourselves to God.

Gloria Gaither

Repentance involves a radical change of heart and mind in which we agree with God's evaluation of our sin and then take specific action to align ourselves with His will.

Henry Blackaby

If we accept His invitation to salvation, we live with Him forever. However, if we do not accept because we refuse His only Son as our Savior, then we exclude ourselves from My Father's House. It's our choice.

Anne Graham Lotz

Today's Prayer

Lord, when I accepted Jesus as my personal Savior, You changed me forever and made me whole. Let me share Your Son's message with my friends, with my family, and with the world. You are a God of love, redemption, conversion, and salvation. I will praise You today and forever. Amen

Beyond Complaining

Be hospitable to one another without complaining.

1 Peter 4:9 HCSB

Most of us have more blessings than we can count, yet we can still find reasons to complain about the minor frustrations of everyday life. To do so, of course, is not only shortsighted, but it is also a serious roadblock on the path to spiritual abundance.

Would you like to feel more comfortable about your circumstances and your life? Then promise yourself that you'll do whatever it takes to ensure that you focus your thoughts and energy on the major blessings you've received (not the minor inconveniences you must occasionally endure).

So the next time you're tempted to complain about the inevitable frustrations of everyday living, don't do it! Today and every day, make it a practice to count your blessings, not your hardships. It's the truly decent way to live.

Gratitude for God's Guidance

Be hospitable to one another without complaining.

1 Peter 4:9 HCSB

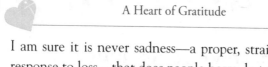
I am sure it is never sadness—a proper, straight, natural response to loss—that does people harm, but all the other things, all the resentment, dismay, doubt and self-pity with which it is usually complicated.

C. S. Lewis

When you're on the verge of throwing a pity party thanks to your despairing thoughts, go back to the Word of God.

Charles Swindoll

It's your choice: you can either count your blessings or recount your disappointments.

Jim Gallery

He wants us to have a faith that does not complain while waiting, but rejoices because we know our times are in His hands—nail-scarred hands that labor for our highest good.

Kay Arthur

Jesus wept, but he never complained.

C. H. Spurgeon

Today's Prayer

Lord, I know that the choice is mine—I can either count my blessings or recount my disappointments. Today, help me to focus my thoughts upon my blessings, my gifts, and my opportunities. Amen

Finding Strength

I am able to do all things through Him who strengthens me.

Philippians 4:13 HCSB

Where do you go to find strength? The gym? The health food store? The espresso bar? There's a better source of strength, of course, and that source is God. He is a never-ending source of strength and courage if you call upon Him.

Are you an energized Christian? You should be. But if you're not, you must seek strength and renewal from the source that will never fail: that source, of course, is your Heavenly Father. And rest assured—when you sincerely petition Him, He will give you all the strength you need to live victoriously for Him.

Have you "tapped in" to the power of God? Have you turned your life and your heart over to Him, or are you muddling along under your own power? The answer to this question will determine the quality of your life here on earth and the destiny of your life throughout all eternity. So start tapping in—and remember that when it comes to strength, God is the Ultimate Source.

Gratitude for God's Protection

Be of good courage, and He shall strengthen your heart, all you who hope in the Lord.

Psalm 31:24 NKJV

Worry does not empty tomorrow of its sorrow; it empties today of its strength.

Corrie ten Boom

When you and I are related to Jesus Christ, our strength and wisdom and peace and joy and love and hope may run out, but His life rushes in to keep us filled to the brim. We are showered with blessings, not because of anything we have or have not done, but simply because of Him.

Anne Graham Lotz

We are never stronger than the moment we admit we are weak.

Beth Moore

Today's Prayer

Lord, whenever I feel discouraged or tired, I will turn to You for strength. I know that when I open my heart to You, Father, You will renew my strength and my enthusiasm. Let Your will be my will, Lord, and let me find my strength in You. Amen

Simplicity Now

But godliness with contentment is a great gain. For we brought nothing into the world, and we can take nothing out. But if we have food and clothing, we will be content with these. But those who want to be rich fall into temptation, a trap, and many foolish and harmful desires, which plunge people into ruin and destruction.

1 Timothy 6:6-9 HCSB

You live in a world where simplicity is in short supply. Think for a moment about the complexity of your everyday life and compare it to the lives of your ancestors. Certainly, you are the beneficiary of many technological innovations, but those innovations have a price: in all likelihood, your world is highly complex. Consider the following:

1. From the moment you wake up in the morning until the time you lay your head on the pillow at night, you are the target of an endless stream of advertising information. Each message is intended to grab your attention in order to convince you to purchase things you didn't know you needed (and probably don't!).

2. Essential aspects of your life, including personal matters such as health care, are subject to an ever-increasing flood of rules and regulations.

3. Unless you take firm control of your time and your life, you may be overwhelmed by an ever-increasing tidal wave of complexity that threatens your happiness.

Your Heavenly Father understands the joy of living simply, and so should you. So do yourself a favor: keep your life as simple as possible. Simplicity is, indeed, genius. By simplifying your life, you are destined to improve it.

Gratitude for God's Guidance

Better a little with the fear of the Lord than great treasure with turmoil.

Proverbs 15:16 HCSB

Nobody is going to simplify your life for you. You've got to simplify things for yourself.

Marie T. Freeman

All that a Christian does, even in eating and sleeping, is prayer, when it is done in simplicity, according to the order of God, without either adding to or diminishing from it by His choice.

John Wesley

It is part of Satan's program to make our faith complicated and involved. Now and then, we need a rediscovery of the simplicity that is in Christ and in our faith in Him.

Vance Havner

Among the enemies to devotion, none is so harmful as distractions. Whatever excites the curiosity, scatters the thoughts, disquiets the heart, absorbs the interests, or shifts our life focus from the kingdom of God within us to the world around us—that is a distraction; and the world is full of them.

A. W. Tozer

The most powerful life is the most simple life. The most powerful life is the life that knows where it's going, that knows where the source of strength is; it is the life that stays free of clutter and happenstance and hurriedness.

Max Lucado

Today's Prayer

Dear Lord, please help me to focus my heart and mind on You and Your love and not to get lost in the jungle of work and technology that takes up the majority of my day. Help me, Father, to find time to be still and sit with You. Amen

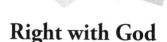

Right with God

Blessed are those who hunger and thirst for righteousness, because they will be filled.

Matthew 5:6 HCSB

How do we live a life that is "right with God"? By accepting God's Son and obeying His commandments. Accepting Christ is a decision that we make one time; following in His footsteps requires thousands of decisions each day.

Whose steps will you follow today? Will you honor God as you strive to follow His Son? Or will you join the lockstep legion that seeks to discover happiness and fulfillment through worldly means? If you are righteous and wise, you will follow Christ. You will follow Him today and every day. You will seek to walk in His footsteps without reservation or doubt. When you do so, you will be "right with God" precisely because you are walking aright with His only begotten Son.

Gratitude for God's Guidance

But the wisdom from above is first pure, then peace-loving, gentle, compliant, full of mercy and good fruits, without favoritism and hypocrisy.

James 3:17 HCSB

Holiness isn't in a style of dress. It's not a matter of rules and regulations. It's a way of life that emanates quietness and rest, joy in family, shared pleasures with friends, the help of a neighbor—and the hope of a Savior.

Joni Eareckson Tada

Holiness has never been the driving force of the majority. It is, however, mandatory for anyone who wants to enter the kingdom.

Elisabeth Elliot

How little people know who think that holiness is dull. When one meets the real thing, it's irresistible.

C. S. Lewis

Our afflictions are designed not to break us but to bend us toward the eternal and the holy.

Barbara Johnson

Today's Prayer

Lord, You are a righteous and Holy God, and You have called me to be a righteous woman. When I fall short, forgive me and renew a spirit of holiness within me. Lead me, Lord, along Your path, and guide me far from the temptations of this world. Let Your Holy Word guide my actions, and let Your love reside in my heart, this day and every day. Amen

Who Rules?

Can you search out the deep things of God? Can you find out the limits of the Almighty? They are higher than heaven—what can you do? Deeper than Sheol—what can you know? Their measure is longer than the earth and broader than the sea.

Job 11:7-9 NKJV

God is sovereign. He reigns over the entire universe and He reigns over your little corner of that universe. Your challenge is to recognize God's sovereignty, to live in accordance with His commandments, and to trust His promises. Sometimes, of course, these tasks are easier said than done.

Your Heavenly Father may not always reveal Himself as quickly (or as clearly) as you would like. But rest assured: God is in control, God is here, and God intends to use you in wonderful, unexpected ways. He desires to lead you along a path of His choosing. Your challenge is to watch, to listen, to learn . . . and to follow. Today.

Gratitude for God's Protection

But the Lord will be a refuge for His people.

Joel 3:16 HCSB

There is something incredibly comforting about knowing that the Creator is in control of your life.

Lisa Whelchel

Nothing happens by happenstance. I am not in the hands of fate, nor am I the victim of man's whims or the devil's ploys. There is One who sits above man, above Satan, and above all heavenly hosts as the ultimate authority of all the universe. That One is my God and my Father!

Kay Arthur

Every experience God gives us, every person he brings into our lives, is the perfect preparation for the future that only he can see.

Corrie ten Boom

You are God's chief creation, and you are here for His pleasure and His glory.

Beth Moore

Today's Prayer

Dear Lord, You are the sovereign God of the universe. You rule over our world, and I will allow You to rule over my heart. I will obey Your commandments, Father, and I will study Your Word. I will seek Your will for my life, and I will allow Your Son to reign over my heart . . . today and every day of my life. Amen

The Power of Optimism

But if we look forward to something we don't have yet, we must wait patiently and confidently.

Romans 8:25 NLT

Pessimism and Christianity don't mix. Why? Because Christians have every reason to be optimistic about life here on earth and life eternal. Mrs. Charles E. Cowman advised, "Never yield to gloomy anticipation. Place your hope and confidence in God. He has no record of failure."

Sometimes, despite our trust in God, we may fall into the spiritual traps of worry, frustration, anxiety, or sheer exhaustion, and our hearts become heavy. What's needed is plenty of rest, a large dose of perspective, and God's healing touch, but not necessarily in that order.

Today, make this promise to yourself and keep it: vow to be a hope-filled Christian. Think optimistically about your life, your profession, and your future. Trust your hopes, not your fears. Take time to celebrate God's glorious creation. And then, when you've filled your heart with hope and gladness, share your optimism with others. They'll be better for it, and so will you. But not necessarily in that order.

A Heart of Gratitude

Make me to hear joy and gladness.

Psalm 51:8 KJV

If you can't tell whether your glass is half-empty or half-full, you don't need another glass; what you need is better eyesight . . . and a more thankful heart.

Marie T. Freeman

The Christian lifestyle is not one of legalistic do's and don'ts, but one that is positive, attractive, and joyful.

Vonette Bright

We may run, walk, stumble, drive, or fly, but let us never lose sight of the reason for the journey, or miss a chance to see a rainbow on the way.

Gloria Gaither

Stop thinking wishfully and start living hopefully.

Emilie Barnes

Today's Prayer

Thank You, Lord, for Your infinite love. Make me an optimistic Christian, Father, as I place my hope and my trust in You. Amen

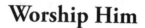

Worship Him

But the hour is coming, and now is, when the true worshipers will worship the Father in spirit and truth; for the Father is seeking such to worship Him. God is Spirit, and those who worship Him must worship in spirit and truth.

John 4:23-24 NKJV

All of mankind is engaged in the practice of worship. Some choose to worship God and, as a result, reap the joy that He intends for His children. Others distance themselves from God by worshiping such things as earthly possessions or personal gratification. …and when they do so, they suffer.

Today, as one way of worshipping God, make every aspect of your life a cause for celebration and praise. Praise God for the blessings and opportunities that He has given you, and live according to the beautiful words found in the 5th chapter of 1 Thessalonians: "Rejoice evermore. Pray without ceasing. In every thing give thanks: for this is the will of God in Christ Jesus concerning you" (vv. 16-18 KJV).

God deserves your worship, your prayers, your praise, and your thanks. And you deserve the joy that is yours when you worship Him with your prayers, with your deeds, and with your life.

A Heart of Gratitude

Happy are those who hear the joyful call to worship, for they will walk in the light of your presence, Lord.

Psalm 89:15 NLT

God actually delights in and pursues our worship (Proverbs 15:8 & John 4:23).

Shirley Dobson

To worship Him in truth means to worship Him honestly, without hypocrisy, standing open and transparent before Him.

Anne Graham Lotz

God asks that we worship Him with our concentrated minds as well as with our wills and emotions. A divided and scattered mind is not effective.

Catherine Marshall

Today's Prayer

Heavenly Father, let today and every day be a time of worship. Let me worship You, not only with words and deeds, but also with my heart. In the quiet moments of the day, let me praise You and thank You for creating me, loving me, guiding me, and saving me. Amen

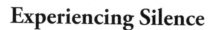

Experiencing Silence

Be silent before Me.

Isaiah 41:1 HCSB

The world seems to grow louder day by day, and our senses seem to be invaded at every turn. If we allow the distractions of a clamorous society to separate us from God's peace, we do ourselves a profound disservice. Our task, as dutiful believers, is to carve out moments of silence in a world filled with noise.

If we are to maintain righteous minds and compassionate hearts, we must take time each day for prayer and for meditation. We must make ourselves still in the presence of our Creator. We must quiet our minds and our hearts so that we might sense God's will and His love.

Has the busy pace of life robbed you of the peace that God has promised? If so, it's time to reorder your priorities and your life. Nothing is more important than the time you spend with your Heavenly Father. So be still and claim the inner peace that is found in the silent moments you spend with God.

A Heart of Gratitude

Truly my soul silently waits for God; from Him comes my salvation.

Psalm 62:1 NKJV

Let your loneliness be transformed into a holy aloneness. Sit still before the Lord. Remember Naomi's word to Ruth: "Sit still, my daughter, until you see how the matter will fall."

Elisabeth Elliot

Because Jesus Christ is our Great High Priest, not only can we approach God without a human "go-between," we can also hear and learn from God in some sacred moments without one.

Beth Moore

In the soul-searching of our lives, we are to stay quiet so we can hear Him say all that He wants to say to us in our hearts.

Charles Swindoll

It is in that stillness that the Voice will be heard, the only voice in all the universe that speaks peace to the deepest part of us.

Elisabeth Elliot

Today's Prayer

Dear Lord, help me remember the importance of silence. Help me discover quiet moments throughout the day so that I can sense Your presence and Your love. Amen

Consider the Possibilities

But Jesus looked at them and said, "With men this is impossible, but with God all things are possible."

Matthew 19:26 HCSB

All of us face difficult days. Sometimes even the most optimistic women can become discouraged, and you are no exception. If you find yourself enduring difficult circumstances, perhaps it's time for an extreme intellectual makeover—perhaps it's time to focus more on your strengths and opportunities, and less on the challenges that confront you. And one more thing: perhaps it's time to put a little more faith in God.

Every day, including this one, is brimming with possibilities. Every day is filled opportunities to grow, to serve, and to share. But if you are entangled in a web of negativity, you may overlook the blessings that God has scattered along your path. So don't give in to pessimism, to doubt, or to cynicism. Instead, keep your eyes upon the possibilities, fix your heart upon the Creator, do your best, and let Him handle the rest.

Gratitude for God's Protection

I will lift up my eyes to the hills—from whence comes my help? My help comes from the Lord, who made heaven and earth.

Psalm 121:1-2 NKJV

God specializes in things fresh and firsthand. His plans for you this year may outshine those of the past. He's prepared to fill your days with reasons to give Him praise.

Joni Eareckson Tada

I could go through this day oblivious to the miracles all around me or I could tune in and "enjoy."

Gloria Gaither

Here lies the tremendous mystery—that God should be all-powerful, yet refuse to coerce. He summons us to cooperation. We are honored in being given the opportunity to participate in His good deeds. Remember how He asked for help in performing His miracles: Fill the water pots, stretch out your hand, distribute the loaves.

Elisabeth Elliot

God specializes in things thought impossible.

Catherine Marshall

Today's Prayer

Lord, as I take the next steps on my life's journey, let me take them with You. Whatever this day may bring, I thank You for the opportunity to live abundantly. Let me lean upon You, Father—and trust You—this day and forever. Amen

Obedience Now

Not everyone who says to Me, "Lord, Lord!" will enter the kingdom of heaven, but the one who does the will of My Father in heaven.

Matthew 7:21 HCSB

God's laws are eternal and unchanging: obedience leads to abundance and joy; disobedience leads to disaster. God has given us a guidebook for righteous living called the Holy Bible. If we trust God's Word and live by it, we are blessed. But, if we choose to ignore God's commandments, the results are as predictable as they are tragic.

Life is a series of decisions and choices. Each day, we make countless decisions that can bring us closer to God... or not. When we live according to God's commandments, we earn for ourselves the abundance and peace that He intends for our lives.

Do you seek God's peace and His blessings? Then obey Him. When you're faced with a difficult choice or a powerful temptation, seek God's counsel and trust the counsel He gives. Invite God into your heart and live according to His commandments. When you do, you will be blessed today, and tomorrow, and forever.

Gratitude for God's Protection

Unless the Lord builds a house, its builders labor over it in vain; unless the Lord watches over a city, the watchman stays alert in vain.

Psalm 127:1 HCSB

Let us never suppose that obedience is impossible or that holiness is meant only for a select few. Our Shepherd leads us in paths of righteousness—not for our name's sake but for His.

Elisabeth Elliot

You may not always see immediate results, but all God wants is your obedience and faithfulness.

Vonette Bright

When life is difficult, God wants us to have a faith that trusts and waits.

Kay Arthur

Today's Prayer

Dear Lord, make me a woman who is obedient to Your Word. Let me live according to Your commandments. Direct my path far from the temptations and distractions of this world. And, let me discover Your will and follow it, Lord, this day and always. Amen

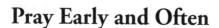

Pray Early and Often

Rejoice always! Pray constantly. Give thanks in everything, for this is God's will for you in Christ Jesus.

1 Thessalonians 5:16-18 HCSB

As the old saying goes, if it's big enough to worry about, it's big enough to pray about. Yet sometimes, we don't pray about the specific details of our lives. Instead, we may offer general prayers that are decidedly heavy on platitudes and decidedly light on particulars.

The next time you pray, try this: be very specific about the things you ask God to do. Of course, God already knows precisely what you need—He knows infinitely more about your life than you do—but you need the experience of talking to your Creator in honest, unambiguous language.

So today, don't be vague with God. Tell Him exactly what you need. He doesn't need to hear the details, but you do.

Gratitude for God's Protection

In the day of my trouble I shall call upon thee, for thou wilt answer me.

Psalm 86:7 KJV

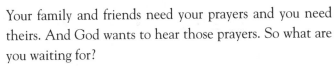
Your family and friends need your prayers and you need theirs. And God wants to hear those prayers. So what are you waiting for?

Marie T. Freeman

God says we don't need to be anxious about anything; we just need to pray about everything.

Stormie Omartian

When the Holy Spirit comes to dwell within us, I believe we gain a built-in inclination to take our concerns and needs to the Lord in prayer.

Shirley Dobson

We must leave it to God to answer our prayers in His own wisest way. Sometimes, we are so impatient and think that God does not answer. God always answers! He never fails! Be still. Abide in Him.

Mrs. Charles E. Cowman

Today's Prayer

Dear Lord, I will be a woman of prayer. I will take everything to You in prayer, and when I do, I will trust Your answers. Amen

Sharing Your Faith

But sanctify the Lord God in your hearts, and always be ready to give a defense to everyone who asks you a reason for the hope that is in you.

1 Peter 3:15 HCSB

Our personal testimonies are extremely important, but sometimes, because of shyness or insecurities, we're afraid to share our experiences. And that's unfortunate.

In his second letter to Timothy, Paul shares a message to believers of every generation when he writes, "God has not given us a spirit of timidity" (1:7). Paul's meaning is clear: When sharing our beliefs, we, as Christians, must be courageous, forthright, and unashamed.

We live in a world that desperately needs the healing message of Christ Jesus. Every believer, each in his or her own way, bears responsibility for sharing the Good News of our Savior.

Billy Graham observed, "Our faith grows by expression. If we want to keep our faith, we must share it." If you are a follower of Christ, the time to express your belief in Him is now. You know how He has touched your heart; help Him do the same for others.

A Heart of Gratitude

I will thank you, Lord, with all my heart; I will tell of all the marvelous things you have done. I will be filled with joy because of you. I will sing praises to your name, O Most High.

Psalm 9:1-2 NLT

There are many timid souls whom we jostle morning and evening as we pass them by; but if only the kind word were spoken they might become fully persuaded.

Fanny Crosby

Your light is the truth of the Gospel message itself as well as your witness as to Who Jesus is and what He has done for you. Don't hide it.

Anne Graham Lotz

There is nothing anybody else can do that can stop God from using us. We can turn everything into a testimony.

Corrie ten Boom

Today's Prayer

Dear Lord, the life that I live and the words that I speak bear testimony to my faith. Make me a faithful servant of Your Son, and let my testimony be worthy of You. Let my words be sure and true, Lord, and let my actions point others to You. Amen

231

Finding Courage

Be strong and courageous, and do the work. Don't be afraid or discouraged, for the Lord God, my God, is with you. He won't leave you or forsake you.

1 Chronicles 28:20 HCSB

Life can be difficult and discouraging at times. During our darkest moments, we can depend upon our friends and family, and upon God. When we do, we find the courage to face even the darkest days with hopeful hearts and willing hands.

Eleanor Roosevelt advised, "You gain strength, courage, and confidence by every great experience in which you really stop to look fear in the face. You are able to say to yourself, 'I lived through this horror. I can take the next thing that comes along.' You must do the thing you think you cannot do."

So the next time you find your courage tested to the limit, remember that you're probably stronger than you think. And remember—with you, your friends, your family and your God all working together, you have nothing to fear.

Gratitude for God's Protection

Be strong and courageous, all you who put your hope in the Lord.

Psalm 31:24 HCSB

Just as courage is faith in good, so discouragement is faith in evil, and, while courage opens the door to good, discouragement opens it to evil.

Hannah Whitall Smith

What is courage? It is the ability to be strong in trust, in conviction, in obedience. To be courageous is to step out in faith—to trust and obey, no matter what.

Kay Arthur

If a person fears God, he or she has no reason to fear anything else. On the other hand, if a person does not fear God, then fear becomes a way of life.

Beth Moore

Today's Prayer

Dear Lord, fill me with Your Spirit and help me face my challenges with courage and determination. Keep me mindful, Father, that You are with me always—and with You by my side, I have nothing to fear. Amen

The Dangers of Pride

Pride comes before destruction, and an arrogant spirit before a fall.

Proverbs 16:18 HCSB

The words from Proverbs 16 remind us that pride and destruction are traveling partners. But as imperfect human beings, we are tempted to puff our chests and crow about our own accomplishments. When we do so, we delude ourselves.

As Christians, we have a profound reason to be humble: We have been refashioned and saved by Jesus Christ, and that salvation came not because of our own good works but because of God's grace. Thus, we are not "self-made"; we are "God-made" and "Christ-saved." How, then, can we be boastful? The answer, of course, is simple: if we are honest with ourselves and with our God, we cannot be boastful. In the quiet moments, when we search the depths of our own hearts, we know that whatever "it" is, God did that. And He deserves the credit.

Gratitude for God's Guidance

Though the Lord is great, he cares for the humble, but he keeps his distance from the proud.

Psalm 138:6 NLT

All kindness and good deeds, we must keep silent. The result will be an inner reservoir of personality power.

Catherine Marshall

We cannot be filled until we are empty. We have to be poor in spirit of ourselves in order to be filled with the Holy Spirit.

Corrie ten Boom

It was as important to me that my children be no more self-righteous than they were unrighteous. In His Gospels, Christ seemed far more tolerant of a repentant sinner than a self-righteous, self-proclaimed saint.

Beth Moore

That's what I love about serving God. In His eyes, there are no little people . . . because there are no big people. We are all on the same playing field. We all start at square one. No one has it better than the other, or possesses unfair advantage.

Joni Eareckson Tada

Today's Prayer

Heavenly Father, Jesus clothed Himself with humility when He chose to come to this earth so that He might live and die for all creation. Christ is my Master and my example. Clothe me with humility, Lord, so that I might be more like Your Son. Amen

On Purpose

I, therefore, the prisoner in the Lord, urge you to walk worthy of the calling you have received.

Ephesians 4:1 HCSB

"What on earth does God intend for me to do with my life?" It's an easy question to ask but, for many of us, a difficult question to answer. Why? Because God's purposes aren't always clear to us. Sometimes we wander aimlessly in a wilderness of our own making. And sometimes, we struggle mightily against God in an unsuccessful attempt to find success and happiness through our own means, not His.

If you're a woman who sincerely seeks God's guidance, He will give it. But, He will make His revelations known to you in a way and in a time of His choosing, not yours, so be patient. If you prayerfully petition God and work diligently to discern His intentions, He will, in time, lead you to a place of joyful abundance and eternal peace.

Sometimes, God's intentions will be clear to you; other times, God's plan will seem uncertain at best. But even on those difficult days when you are unsure which way to turn, you must never lose sight of these overriding facts: God created you for a reason; He has important work for you to do; and He's waiting patiently for you to do it.

And the next step is up to you.

Gratitude for God's Guidance

You will show me the path of life; in Your presence is fullness of joy; at Your right hand are pleasures forevermore.

Psalm 16:11 NKJV

His life is our light—our purpose and meaning and reason for living.

Anne Graham Lotz

Yesterday is just experience but tomorrow is glistening with purpose—and today is the channel leading from one to the other.

Barbara Johnson

Only God's chosen task for you will ultimately satisfy. Do not wait until it is too late to realize the privilege of serving Him in His chosen position for you.

Beth Moore

Today's Prayer

Dear Lord, I know that You have a purpose for my life, and I will seek that purpose today and every day that I live. Let my actions be pleasing to You, and let me share Your Good News with a world that so desperately needs Your healing hand and the salvation of Your Son. Amen

Give Him Your Heart

For God so loved the world that He gave His only begotten Son, that whoever believes in Him should not perish but have everlasting life.

John 3:16 NKJV

Your decision to allow Christ to reign over your heart is the pivotal decision of your life. It is a decision that you cannot ignore. It is a decision that is yours and yours alone.

God's love for you is deeper and more profound than you can imagine. God's love for you is so great that He sent His only Son to this earth to die for your sins and to offer you the priceless gift of eternal life. Now, you must decide whether or not to accept God's gift. Will you ignore it or embrace it? Will you accept Christ's love and build a lifelong relationship with Him, or will you turn away from Him and take a different path?

Accept God's gift now: allow His Son to preside over your heart, your thoughts, and your life, starting this very instant.

A Heart of Gratitude

For the Lord is good. His unfailing love continues forever, and his faithfulness continues to each generation.

Psalm 100:5 NLT

It's your heart that Jesus longs for:
your will to be made His own
with self on the cross forever,
and Jesus alone on the throne.

—

Ruth Bell Graham

The amount of power you experience to live a victorious, triumphant Christian life is directly proportional to the freedom you give the Spirit to be Lord of your life!

Anne Graham Lotz

Choose Jesus Christ! Deny yourself, take up the Cross, and follow Him—for the world must be shown. The world must see, in us, a discernible, visible, startling difference.

Elisabeth Elliot

Jesus is the personal approach from the unseen God coming so near that he becomes inescapable. You don't have to find him—you just have to consent to be found.

E. Stanley Jones

And because we know Christ is alive, we have hope for the present and hope for life beyond the grave.

Billy Graham

Today's Prayer

Dear God, conform me to Your image. Create in me a new heart—a heart reflects the love that You lavish upon me. Let Your love and wisdom shine through me, so that others will see Your will at work in my heart and my life. Amen